Praise for *Born Jumping*

"Simply stated, this is an essential handbook for today's entrepreneurs—gritty, shockingly honest and 100% real. *Born Jumping* is an astounding blend of heart, head and spirit that delivers practical advice and an intimate portrait of success."

—Jon LoDuca, Founder, The Wisdom Link, Inc.
and author of *Wisdom Driven*

"Benjamin Genet has more character in his little finger than most people have in their entire bodies. In this remarkable guide to successful living, Ben shows you what success really requires."

—Michael Levin, *New York Times* best selling author

AF334863

BORN JUMPING

Benjamin Genet

Copyright © 2013 by Benjamin Genet

All rights reserved. No part of this book may be used or reproduced in any manner whatsoever without prior written consent of the publisher except in the case of brief quotations embodied in critical articles and reviews. Special book excerpts or customized printings can be created to fit specific needs.

For information contact:
Genet Property Group
Benjamin Genet
ben@genetgroup.com

Library of Congress Control Number: 2013919524

ISBN PB: 978-1-9397582-9-3
ISBN HC: 978-1-9397582-7-9
ISBN eBook: 978-1-9397582-8-6

Printed in the United States of America

Contents

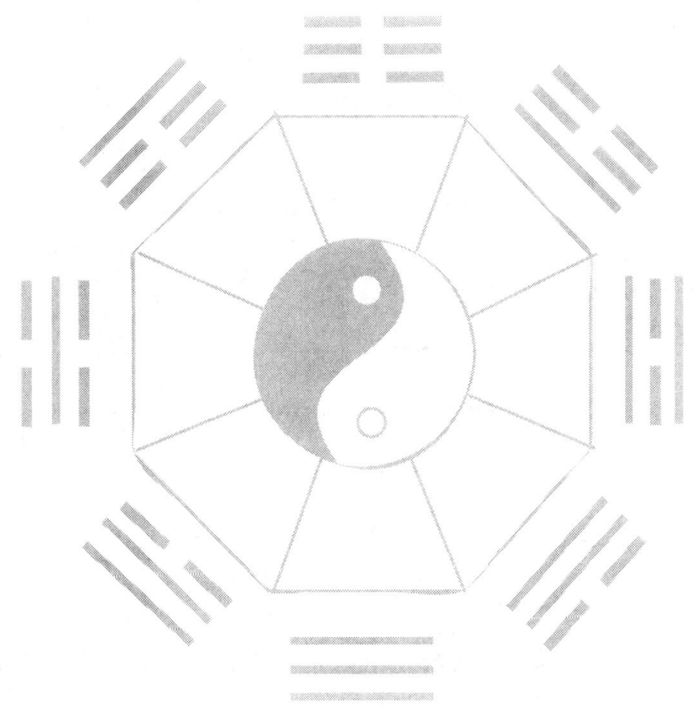

Dedication

Born Jumping was written for three groups of people.

First and foremost, it is for my children, so that when they become adults, they may better understand me, and know that I want them to live an impassioned life of honor. I want them to engage the world—to be proactive, not reactive. I want them to spend their time in things that move them. I want them to be charitable and honest and good. I believe that living a life of honor will make you happier and make more room for love in your life—and I want my children to know that I tried to do all these things with every bit of ability that I had, that I never stop trying to improve even though I constantly screw it up, and I love them very, very deeply.

It is for entrepreneurs and those who wish to become entrepreneurs, and those who want to be intentional about the quest for success in life. I want people to be able to visualize where they want to go and really try to get there, knowing full well that what they're doing is the right thing, and that it will make their lives better and improve those of everyone around them.

Lastly, it is for the young adult with A.D.H.D., and his or her parents. The skills explored in this book will help you use your A.D.H.D.—your blessing—to your advantage.

I dedicate this book to my wife, Dorit, who had the confidence in me when I didn't, and who allowed me to fail many times. For her, believing in me came easy. And for me, her belief enabled me to do great things. Without opening yourself to the risk of failure, great success cannot be attained.

✦✦✦

When I received my black belt in Tora Dojo Karate, the certificate included this powerful dictate:

Be firm and unyielding against evil. Demonstrate the strength of your will and your purpose. Let unremitting energy and untiring effort be the hallmark of your development. Be humble and modest, taking extreme care to use your powers only for the greater good. Maintain and preserve strict observance of the laws of your discipline.

Struggle. Dare to be great. Jump right in.

It is not the critic who counts; not the man who points out how the strong man stumbles, or where the doer of deeds could have done them better. The credit belongs to the man who is actually in the arena, whose face is marred by dust and sweat and blood; who strives valiantly; who errs, who comes short again and again, because there is no effort without error and shortcoming; but who does actually strive to do the deeds; who knows great enthusiasms, the great devotions; who spends himself in a worthy cause; who at the best knows in the end the triumph of high achievement, and who at the worst, if he fails, at least fails while daring greatly, so that his place shall never be with those cold and timid souls who neither know victory nor defeat.

— Theodore Roosevelt,
Citizenship in a Republic, 1910

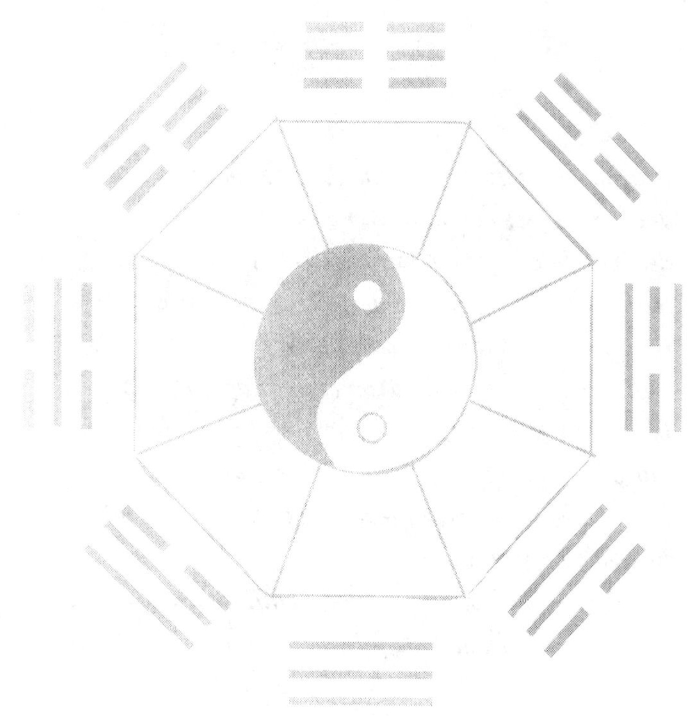

Introduction

Walking "The Way"

FOR MANY YEARS, A martial arts grand master named Professor Sober was my teacher. The topics we covered ranged from Eastern philosophy to karate, from meditation to life, and everything in between. When I was a college student, I spent three nights a week for two summers in his dojo with him and thirty other students, studying energy and meditation. He used to tell us this story about a good-looking guy who had once walked into his dojo:

"Professor, I want to study martial arts."

"Well, how do you feel?" asked Professor Sober.

"Great," said the guy confidently.

"How is your family?"

"Wonderful," he responded.

"Are you married?"

"Yes, I married my high school sweetheart."

"Do you fight with her?" the Professor asked.

"No."

"Do you get along with your parents?"

"Yes, always!" said the guy.

"What do you do for a living?"

"I'm a doctor."

"Did you always want to be a doctor?"

"Yes."

Professor Sober said to the guy, "Get the hell out of my dojo."

I've always loved this story. His point was basic: if you weren't troubled and ripped up inside, struggling and searching for something in life, then you wouldn't need what he had to offer. It was a valuable lesson for me, and that attitude has a lot to do with this book. There are lots of passionate people—like myself and many of you—who continue to seek more, no matter where they find themselves. We derive satisfaction from the quest itself. Upon reaching the goal, we often feel a bit empty inside, because we have no other goals to pursue.

The modern translation of the Chinese word "dojo" is "parking lot," "arena," or "martial arts school." The ancient meaning of the derivative word for "dojo," "doja," however, was a "place to which you went to confront and drive out your demons." Everyone has demons. Some ignore them. For the person who wants to challenge them, I welcome you into my dojo. For me, and for all entrepreneurs, the business world is the dojo, and the tools you can obtain from this book are your weapons to use as you battle on your quest for success.

I'm a financially successful real estate investor and property manager in southern Florida. In addition to a multitude of commercial and residential properties, I have a wife who loves me, a black belt in karate, and a great family and community. These are all blessings that I'm deeply grateful for. I also have A.D.D. (attention deficit disorder). Needless to say, I've had my ups and downs in life, and it wasn't so long ago that I was just a scared kid who wasn't able to study in school.

When I was ten, my brother died in a skydiving accident. From that moment on, I realized how unexpected and difficult life could be. My mother, understandably, lost herself in sorrow, thereby denying me and my brother David of some much-needed attention. I became a boat whose tether was let go. I graduated from a mediocre elementary school, and my parents decided to send me to a private boarding school in New York. I remember showing up without even a pen or notebook in hand.

There's a very big difference between being extremely intelligent and being a good student, and most of the kids at the boarding school were both—I, on the other hand, was never a great student. Each night at boarding school, I wandered around the dorm causing trouble, a fourteen-year-old boy with A.D.D., trying to figure out what the hell I was supposed to do while everybody else was studying.

I did spend my senior year of high school in Israel, and there, I was able to begin to come into my own. It was a great experience for me, and soon, it helped me gain great confidence. In college, I made a name for myself for the first time. I had good friends, I loved the wrestling team, and I always felt popular. I finally had found my place. A few times throughout my college career, I rented out clubs and threw "for-profit" parties in them. At the first party, I made $4,000, and it felt great. That was my entrepreneurial streak kicking in. In law school, I was still incapable of studying, but I paid attention and went to class. I enjoyed much of that experience. I somehow managed to get C+'s and graduated in the middle third of my class—the bottom of the middle third, but still, the middle third. That's who I was.

I'm fifty-one years old now. I've been married for twenty-five years to the same wonderful woman, and my marriage has never been better. It was rough-going for some time, but I'm improving a lot. So is my wife, but she didn't have as far to go as I did. Our children love us, and even though my relationships with them are not perfect, they want to be with me and I want to be with them. My business is thriving— I've purchased almost thirty real estate deals since I started. I still get petrified when I'm buying a new big deal, but I love it. I have great relationships, great investors who trust me, and I am very proud of myself. The success I have—in my relationships, in my career, in my personal pursuits—is success I've had to work at and fight for every step of the way, but that work has brought me far, and it's that fight that I love.

When it comes to stepping into the dojo of life and fighting for what I want, I jump right in. Hell, I was born jumping. I wake up in the morning and I need to do something. I can't sit still. I'm always looking, always hunting, always striving to be better. There are opportunities for success everywhere, if you know where and how to look. I've invested in real estate, stocks, commercial lending, and many start-up companies. I love the smell of the deal. It just turns me on. In fact, the attraction I feel to the deal is stronger than the appeal of the money. Sometimes this desire clouds my judgment and I lose. And sometimes, this desire gives me courage to go into deals that others would not touch. It's allowed me to live a large life—a life beyond the expectations I had for myself as a young man. And I've learned from it. Life is about living the journey and the quest for success, not the arrival.

I believe that by engaging my life with focused intention, discipline, attention to positivity, and constant protection from the controlling nature of negativity, the quests I accept will be filled with triumph. In this book, you'll learn how to channel these techniques. They'll guide you in achieving the most powerful state of mind in the universe, commonly referred to by many Eastern philosophies as "The Way."

The Way, in short, is the great secret to success. Walking The Way will help you live a life filled with purpose, meaning, and personal success, however you may define it. I'll show you how to use everything you already have to Walk The Way. You'll use it all to make it happen for yourself: your relationships (good and bad), your wisdom, your failures and successes, your fears and your confidence, your patience and impulsiveness, your self-centeredness and your gratitude, your generosity, your ambition—every single facet that is unique to you. We'll combine it with what I call the Jumper's Success Formula, and the results will astound you. I will teach you to be a Warrior of Light and educate you on the techniques, mindset, and actions that enable you to tap into the most powerful secret mankind has ever known.

The Warrior of the Light

Every Warrior of the Light has felt afraid of going into battle.

Every Warrior of the Light has, at some time in the past, lied or betrayed someone.

Every Warrior of the Light has trodden a path that was not his.

Every Warrior of the Light has suffered for the most trivial of reasons.

Every Warrior of the Light has, at least once, believed that he was not a Warrior of the Light.

Every Warrior of the Light has failed in his spiritual duties.

Every Warrior of the Light has said "yes" when he wanted to say "no."

Every Warrior of the Light has hurt someone he loved.

That is why he is a Warrior of the Light, because he has been through all this and yet has never lost hope of being better than he is.

—Paulo Coelho

WARRIORS OF LIGHT

If one can truly embrace "The Way," it is by freeing the mind of clutter. We must accept the fact that we don't have control over our ultimate destination and realize that we're all just specks in a universe that we can't even comprehend. Why, then, even bother? Why bother trying to become financially profitable, or having a fantastic relationship, or trying to get invited to fun barbecues and spend time with great people? Why try to win every race you enter?

Personally, I bother because I love it. I love the struggle, and I love the life I lead in the world of American Capitalism. I love making money. I don't spend my time meditating in a cave or under a waterfall somewhere in ancient China. I value the personal freedoms of my great country, and accomplishing something I set out to do is what fuels me. I love being an entrepreneur and a capitalist with the power to use my success to do good. I love being a human animal created by the divine. I was born to struggle, to fail and achieve, and I will make no apologies for that. I revel in the pursuit of success. I am filled with primal desires: leading my pack, feeding ravenously, protecting my mate and children, procreating.

I didn't always love it. Like so many of you, I've searched for God and spiritual growth, and I've tried to find my place in this world. I've been on a quest. I didn't know why I was unhappy and lonely. Out of necessity, I eventually was able to open myself up to some emotionally penetrating philosophies—the primary of which is that this lifetime of ours will end relatively soon. We're here now, and what we have will end, regardless of the potential existence of an afterlife of some sort. The unification with the energy source of the universe is the singular goal, but the salvation must come from the quest itself. When I can wholly internalize this, I'm on my game, and there is no inner conflict. The challenge is to be able to maintain that center. This is the great struggle, the ultimate goal, and this is the state of mind that we call "The Way."

This book deals with the importance of that struggle and the great value that can be derived from it. More profoundly, as a Warrior of Light, you will learn how to embrace the struggle. Unification with the energy of the universe is the optimal state of being. Acting from this centeredness, combined with confidence and a clear purpose, will ultimately lead to worldly success and deep spiritual satisfaction.

HOW TO READ THIS BOOK

When you read this book, I want you to focus on the concepts that surround the actions listed, as opposed to just the actions themselves. There are many types of practices and techniques that you could apply to improve your personal and/or entrepreneurial life. In the following chapters, we will discuss the practices and techniques that I have found to be most significant for me. That should absolutely not diminish other ideas that work for you. Use what you have. Search for new concepts. Never tire in this pursuit.

What I'm really after here is to somehow engage you in the "how and why" of what you've chosen to do. This "how and why" brings all the senses of your being into what you're doing. It makes you intentional. If you go to a networking event and you just sit there—well, sure, you attended a networking event, but to no benefit; you didn't accomplish anything. If you understand your purpose for being there, though—the "how and why"—it will lead to more successful behavior. You'll engage people in a productive and compelling way and leave them wanting more of you, which is what networking is all about. That's the end game in any scenario:

to come away from the effort with something tangible. That possibility is always there. You just need to seek it out and make it yours.

Bear in mind that the techniques and practices you'll find here—like networking, charitable efforts, and expressing your gratitude—are ineffective without a significant amount of **intention, discipline, focus,** and your own philosophical and moral **code of conduct.** I call these four concepts **The Jumper's Success Formula.** When they're combined, these components become the power behind every action taken, and the results are consequently intensified. That's what we're trying to accomplish: to maximize the results of our actions to reach our next lofty goal.

These techniques will always work. They're tried and true—not just by me, but by many. I got these practices from a lifetime of learning: from Hermann Hesse and Richard Bach, Dan Millman and Ayn Rand, Alan Lubarr and Professor Sober; the list goes on. As you read this book, understand that this is simply a collection of practices that, if applied, will work and work well. You will build character and you will be successful as you learn to balance being a Warrior of Light.

◆◆◆

I don't have any "facts" for you. I just have my experiences. I use real estate to teach these lessons for success because it's the only business I know. Whether you're selling shoes, televisions, or carpeting, you're investing money in a product. Your time is also an investment; it's in limited supply, and it needs to be used efficiently. Managing your investments is a core component in any business. My particular investment is all about real estate, but the wisdom gleaned from my experiences can be applied to the pursuit of any goal, personal or entrepreneurial: building a business, getting a girlfriend, or making friends.

I've never been satisfied. There have certainly been periods of my life when I've been happy, but I've never been satisfied. My ambition and my insecurity both drive me forward!

This book is for people who want more, whether it be love, attention, money, spiritual growth, or getting invited to better barbecues. This book is for people who, like Siddhartha, the man who became the Buddha, are on a personal quest. If Siddhartha had been happy and satisfied being a prince with loving parents, he wouldn't have spent his life struggling and climbing to become Enlightened. Ultimately, his trials and tribulations were what helped Siddhartha achieve Nirvana. I don't believe I will ever reach Nirvana, but I sure as hell won't stop clawing my way to the top. I revel in the struggle to get there, and if you're with me, then this book is for you.

Via

Ship To

Market ID: 76524080
Order ID: 1307036
Order Date: 07/06/2026
Shipping Method:

Alibris APEX DC 76524080-64
APEX
800 AVONDALE AVE.
GRANDVIEW HEIGHTS, OH 43212-3473, US

SKU	QTY	TITLE	TOTAL
BSM.14VUZ	1	Born Jumping	9.32

Order Total: $9.32

Your order has been packaged and created with great care. Enjoy! Bay State Books

chapter 1

The Jumper's Success Formula

It is better by noble boldness to run the risk of being subject to half of the evils we anticipate than to remain in cowardly listlessness for fear of what might happen.
—Herodotus

IMAGINE TWO EQUALLY STRONG people throwing the same punch with the same physical force. One has spent a lifetime developing Chi (internal energy), and one has just focused on physical strength. The man who has spent his lifetime learning how to generate internal energy would deliver a punch that would cause a significantly greater impact on the universe than the man just throwing a powerful punch. Without the energy component, the second punch is less influential.

You can think of this energy component as an operating system for success; you can plug it into anything you do. Everyone has this power inside themselves. Most spend their lifetimes complaining about what stopped them. I suggest spending your lifetime harnessing and strengthening this great power. It will improve not only your own life, but that of those around you as well. There are many ways to develop this energy, this Chi, but each technique involves some semblance of **intention**, **discipline**, **focus**, and your **code of conduct**—the four components of our **Jumper's Success Formula.** If Walking The Way is the secret to success, then the Jumper's Success Formula is a technique for Walking The Way, and we will apply it to each and every thing we do.

JUMPER'S
success formula

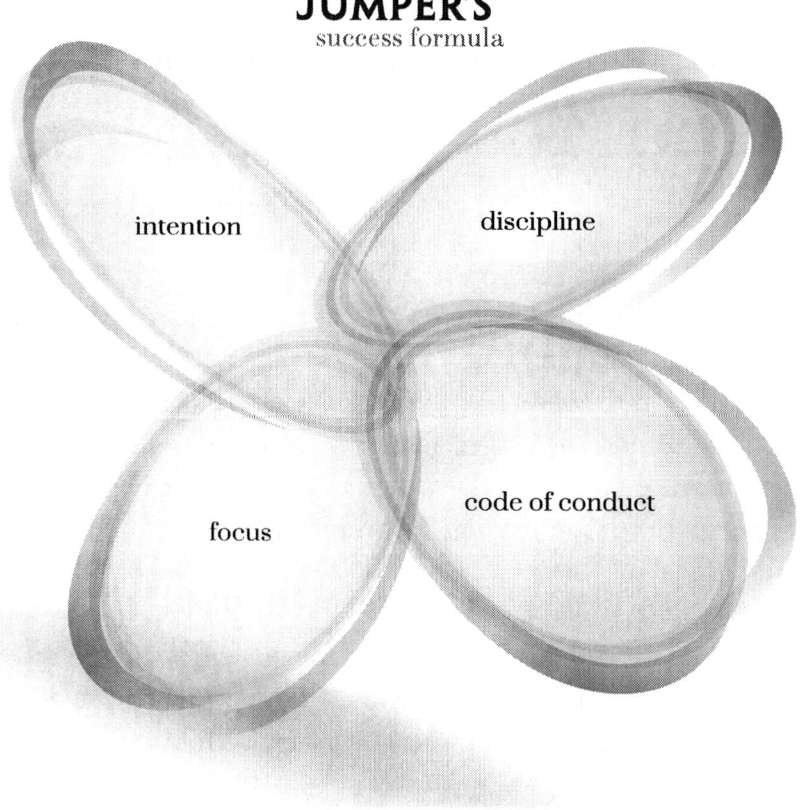

INTENTION

Intention is the first of the four components. It is the GPS of our four-pronged structure—it helps determine where we are going in life. When we define success, or decide we're committed to something, it is by activating **intention**. Whether it's impressing that pretty girl across the room, getting another dollar on your financial statement, or going to that great party with the most ambitious and intelligent people around, it's where we ultimately want to be. Intention is also the first layer to be applied to every activity that we undertake.

Intention is the vision behind the action. It is a combination of what you want, where you want to go, why you want to go there, and what "reaching the goal" means to you. All these elements are combined to propel you forward and make your present activity more purposeful. Keep the future in mind, and it will inform and improve everything you do in your present. Consciously adding intention to your life is the difference between having a race car with regular unleaded gas and a race car with rocket fuel—that punch with internal energy, and the punch without. We must constantly work at improving, understanding, and maintaining it in order to reach our goals.

To be intentional is to know what you want and where you are going. What's your ultimate goal? Be future-focused. If you have a job selling sneakers and you like getting paid eleven dollars an hour, your intention is just to sell sneakers. But if you own a store that sells sneakers, and you sell someone those sneakers with the intention of having a wildly successful store that provides for you, then selling that pair takes on a wholly different meaning. You want the store to be financially successful, and have repeat customers, and you want to be able to take the profits and buy a house for your family or pay for your children's weddings or build a retirement nest egg. That doesn't mean that the intentional man with big goals can't hire the employee with small goals, but it does mean that the drive in the two men is not the same, and therefore the ability to sell the sneakers might not be the same, either. Without that constant desire to grow, it won't be about seeing what shoe styles sell better, or bringing people into the store, or making your customers love you and want to come back. It will only be about selling that one pair. Carry your ultimate motivation in everything you do, and that punch will be harder and faster.

DISCIPLINE

Discipline is knowing what you want and doing something about it.
—Michael Andron

Once you've taken the step and identified your intention, you have to make a commitment to it. **Discipline** is that commitment. If your goal is to lose weight but you don't diet or exercise, your commitment to that goal is obviously weak. Someone who is focused trains hard, commits to the intention, and is preoccupied with the goal. Discipline is the preparation, mental and physical, required in advance to help maintain your focus on your intention.

Why is it that the lucky breaks always happen to the athletes that practice the hardest? Those athletes are disciplined. Discipline is the emotional and psychological commitment to stay on track and get where your intention wants to go. You cannot run a marathon unless you consistently train for it. Giving up sleeping in on Saturday mornings to run ten miles requires discipline. Not eating or drinking too much so you can wake up and run the next morning requires discipline.

We must always give up a lot to achieve a goal. Discipline can be taught, but then we must train ourselves to be disciplined. I don't always want to read *The Wall Street Journal* or *The Economist* or *BusinessWeek*, but as a businessman, if I don't read them, then I'm not current, I'm not as sharp, and I might miss an opportunity. Without the required discipline, I won't be able to act on the opportunity that pops up, if I notice it at all.

In Jiu Jitsu, we practice a figure-eight move to use when someone lunges at you. You put your right hand over their left, then pivot on your left foot and twist behind them. Miraculously, you wind up standing directly behind the person with your hand on their throat, and you're in complete control. This is a basic but difficult move that you practice for years to achieve the right nuances.

A few years ago, I was at a wedding where I was horsing around with a friend of my nephew. He was twenty-five years old, big, strong, and, at that time, drunk. I don't remember exactly what happened, but I do know that he ultimately lunged at me, and my instinct was to react with that move. In a flash, I was behind him and had him by the throat before I really knew what had happened. The only reason I could react that way is that I went to Jiu Jitsu for fifteen years and rarely missed a practice; I was disciplined. I practiced it in the morning. I practiced when I was tired. I practiced it when I was fresh. Years later, this opportunity arose, and I was fully prepared for it.

Set up a plan and train hard. Train yourself to be disciplined, and then train yourself to follow through with that commitment to your intention. This is a must. There is no way around it, but the results from this one behavior will far exceed the effort, and your life will be forever enhanced.

FOCUS

How can we take the grand, philosophical ideas surrounding our intention and apply them to our present? We've got discipline, but we also need to **focus** on our goals to help maintain our commitment. Often, we are driving on the highway and we barely remember the drive—only that we got there. We drove safely, and we were so focused on where we were going that we blocked out everything else around us. That focus is crucial. When a batter is facing a pitcher, the ultimate goal is to win the game. At the second when the pitch is coming in, though, the batter has to be completely and solely focused on hitting the ball. Nothing else can be of import.

That shoe-selling entrepreneur might want to open multiple stores, but he had better be focused on that one sneaker sale first. Sometimes, there's a chain of focus. He's got to be focused on the store being clean, on making sure his air conditioner works, on having employees who will greet the customer in a friendly fashion. And then, he's got to be sure that the sale is carried out and that the customer is truly happy. That kind of singular focus will allow for grander goals.

When I was learning Kata (a sequence of movements in Karate), my teacher Michael would always ask me what the most important move in the Kata was. Michael's answer? "The most important move in the Kata is the one you are currently doing!" In order to end up in the correct stance, each move has to be precise. Each move requires all my focus.

Apply that kind of focus to everything you do. Your stance won't be precise at the end if you don't focus on the moves that get you there. Your focus will also attract other people to you. They'll know you are serious about what you're trying to accomplish, and the intensity of your focus and the discipline that you bring to it will give you more credibility.

While it is crucial that you focus on each step, make sure that your ultimate goal is the real focal point. Don't get so carried away working at the minutiae at hand that you lose sight of the endpoint. Your focus on the minutiae exists because of your focus on the goal. Writing this book is a lot of fun, but if I didn't commit to its conclusion, it would never get done. I need to focus on multiple tasks: each sentence, each paragraph, each chapter, and the book as a whole. Focus without intention might be a big waste of time, but intention without focus is a recipe for mediocrity.

It's not easy to balance the two. If you're trying to focus on the minutiae to the exclusion of other things, how, then, are you to focus on multiple big pictures simultaneously? Unfortunately, life will require that effort of you—there are always conflicting energies whirling around at the same time. What you can do to help yourself is **practice**. Remember discipline? We can train ourselves to commit to more than one thing at a time.

Another technique—my personal savior—is to try and **compartmentalize and prioritize**. I focus on the big picture

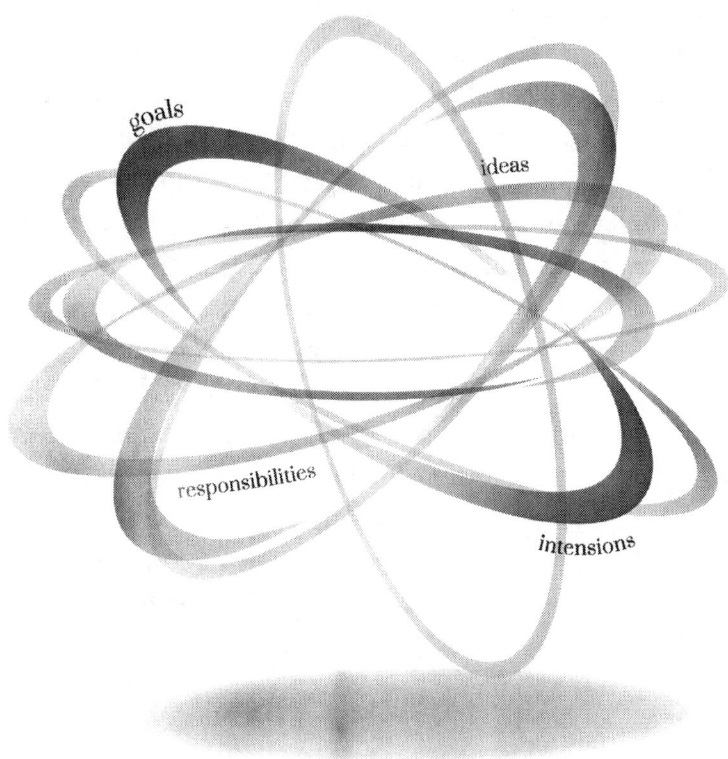

in some situations and the small picture in others, and it's up to me to determine what each situation requires of me. As long as I'm prepared to focus on anything, I can shift through these issues and perform at my best.

As you begin to apply focus to your life, you'll find that you do need to use it for many things at once. You can focus on your family while training for your black belt, and at the same time, focus on growing a chain of sneaker stores. Learning to focus takes discipline and practice. Your work on this will constantly change as you grow. Do not ever stop training and improving. This process will infect every other activity in your life, and you'll be more competent at everything you do. That's a big promise I'm making to you, but you'll find that it's true if you work hard.

Why is it that so many young people that are champions in one area of their lives can reinvent themselves and be great at something else? The answer is that they use the same qualities that made them great in one area of life to propel them in their next endeavor. They have carefully and diligently acquired these practiced and refined traits. It's not in the "what," but in the "how" they do what they do.

Be cognizant that focus is not limited to an immediate act or a particular goal; focus must be applied to anything you want to accomplish, whether it's making the world a better place, improving your relationship, or seeking to profit in your business. Focus is the moment of impact. Think about the concept of prayer without focus. If you focus on the omnipotent divine while praying, and you have blinders on to everything else around you, how powerful will that moment be?

CODE OF CONDUCT

Your personal code of conduct is the set of laws by which you live your life. It's about integrity. It's about what you value. It's about how you treat people. It's crucial that you define this for yourself, because it will affect both your goals and your interactions with the world as a whole. It determines who you are. How else can we begin to define ourselves without a moral set of rules? Find a way to hold yourself accountable. Find ways to let your integrity shine through. I've spent a lifetime working through and understanding my own code of conduct, and perhaps it will help you begin to define yours.

Personally, I want to be one of the good guys. I want to be kind. I want to be a good father and a good husband. I want to know that I've done the right thing and that I'm making the world a better place. This is important to me. This is how I was educated. This was influenced not only by those who positively taught me to be a better person, but also by my own negative moral lapses in judgment *and* of those around me. I don't want those lapses. I am focused, disciplined, and filled with the intent to fight off my own desires if they are detrimental to morality. I want to be rich, but I will not steal or cheat. I will be honest. I will volunteer my time to help those less fortunate. This is the basis for my code of conduct, and it is present in every success I've had, small or great.

A large portion of my code of conduct stems from my upbringing. I was raised in a very entrepreneurial family— my grandparents owned their own business, and my mother was always buying various pieces of real estate for profit. My father was entrepreneurial, too, but his ambition waned over time. When I was ten, my brother and I would melt crayons on Coca-Cola bottles and sell them to people living on our block. So my business sense and my drive for success come from that upbringing.

My need to be a good parent comes from the same upbringing, but it stems from one of those lapses in judgment. My mother was a great caretaker to those who were sick and obviously needed help. I had scarlet fever as a kid, and my fever skyrocketed to 106 degrees. My mother brought a mattress into my room and she slept on the floor next to me, and she put cold compresses on me all day and night until I got better. But when I was physically healthy and struggling in school because of my A.D.D., the most she could do was send me to boarding school instead of hiring a tutor for me or getting to the root of the problem that we didn't understand. I don't want that for my children. I want to be an active and engaged parent who is always there for them, and I won't be satisfied with myself if I'm not.

Liking yourself is so important for your true self-esteem, and doing the right thing goes a long way towards liking yourself. You're not just doing right by others; you're doing right by yourself. If you maintain your integrity, you maintain ease in your own life. Keep it up front and visible. That way, you set a standard for interactions for both you and others, in business and in your personal life.

When renting a warehouse to someone, I always tell them first that they're required to pay for their own garbage and fix their own garage doors and air conditioning if they break. That's my integrity at the forefront, and it creates fewer misunderstandings. When trying to make a sale, it's unusual and ill-advised to explain the difficulties in doing business with you to the customer. I believe, though, that by bringing these issues to the forefront instead of hiding them in the fine print in the lease (where they remain anyway), I can avoid significant problems with the customer in the future. If I explain everything at the beginning of the relationship with a tenant, the basis of the relationship then becomes *honesty*. Getting a new customer is far more expensive than keeping an old one. Liars and cheats have to keep finding new investors, new girlfriends, and new relationships time after time.

I've certainly made mistakes and lost tenants due to misunderstandings. These are scenarios to learn from, and with each relationship I begin, I try harder to keep my code of conduct at the forefront. Living with integrity minimizes hassles, which ultimately increases productivity. I spend less time on back-end problems and more time doing deals, going fishing, or spending time with my family. Integrity also separates you from the majority that find excuses to override their moral code. This is being a Warrior of Light.

The thousands of ways your integrity will affect you when you're not around are even more profound. A pared-down definition of this might be reputation. If I'm away on vacation but I suddenly need a new air conditioner in one of my properties, my air conditioner guy, Norman, will install it even if I'm not there to sign a contract or give him a deposit,

because our relationship is built on trust. If I mess someth
up at work with one of my employees, I can apologize and
they'll know I mean it, because they trust me. If my wife
walks into the gym and sees me talking to some pretty girl
on the elliptical next to me, my wife says, "Hi! I'm Dorit,"
and doesn't want to kill me, because she trusts me. How people perceive you is a direct reflection on how you live your
life and the moral code that you follow.

We are all tempted, at times, to blur the lines of honesty in order to benefit ourselves personally or financially.
Bear in mind, though, that the benefits of living in the light
far exceed the short-term benefits of being a slime bag. The
benefits come back to you constantly. Overcome your short-term desires and do the right thing.

THE ESSENCE

The four components of the Jumper's Success Formula
are truly the essence of this book and, I believe, the essence
of a successful and fulfilled life. For anyone who is pushing
the envelope on a personal or entrepreneurial quest, this formula is armor, sword, and shield. It will keep you safe, cut
through the destruction and negativity you invariably will
encounter, and keep you on the road to success. Apply this
formula to the rest of the techniques in this book, and use
it as a guide for other endeavors in your life. Work hard at
developing these skills. Practice relentlessly.

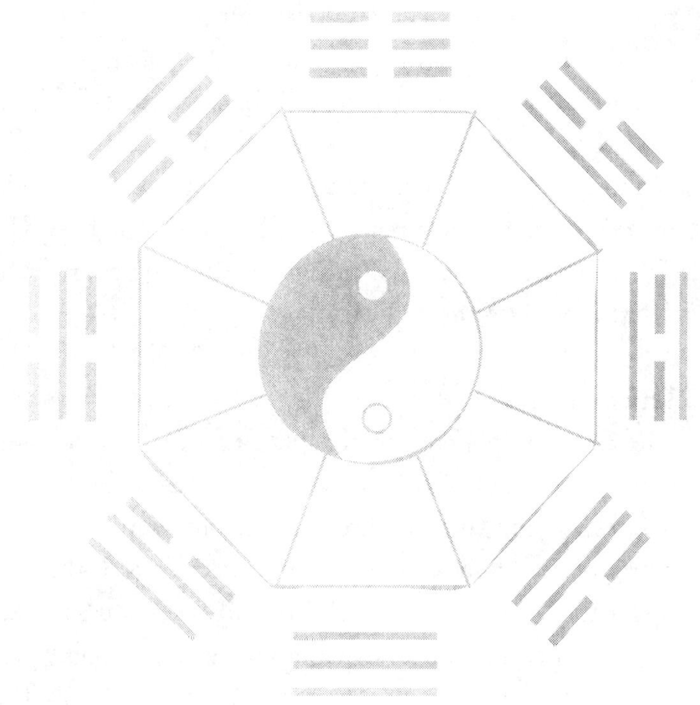

chapter 2

Embrace the Power of Intention

Find a purpose in life so big it will challenge every capacity to be at your best.
—David O. McKay

WHEN I WAS TWENTY-SIX, my perspective on life shifted drastically. I had just gotten married, my wife was working two jobs, and I'd flunked the bar exam. I was married to this exceptional, beautiful woman who looked at me with these big blue eyes and thought I was amazing, but I felt like a complete phony. I didn't see how I could possibly deserve the love of someone like her—when I looked in the mirror, all I saw was just another guy who talked the talk (and boy, did I!) and feared growing up.

I wanted to do the right thing, but I didn't know how to do it or where to turn for help. I was in deep despair, which made me a terrible husband. My dojo—the arena filled with demons to face—was my entire life of going into business, and there was nowhere to hide from it.

I tried many different ways to get myself out of my non-productive hole. I tried selling commercial and residential real estate. I tried importing shoes from China and selling them to the Caribbean. I tried selling insurance door-to-door in middle-class neighborhoods. When I finally passed the bar exam, I tried working as an underpaid lawyer for a mediocre attorney in South Florida. I always met the licensing requirements and put out what I thought was the required amount of effort. The problem was, I never felt any passion.

Ultimately, I opened a law practice. I spent most of my time bringing in business. There were parts of it I did enjoy, but as time went on, I realized that I wanted to be the client instead. Sometime during my "lawyer stage," I befriended my brother's friend Eric, who built warehouses for a living. We'd go out to lunch, and I would spend the whole time bemoaning my life as a lawyer. His response was always the same: "Screw law; build warehouses." Finally, I took Eric's advice: I did my research, found an investor, and built my first warehouse. Looking back, it all seems so easy, but it took me years to get to where I needed to be to get it done.

At the same time as the construction of my warehouse, the real estate market crashed. I took the opportunity to buy a deeply discounted commercial property from the FDIC that had been foreclosed. The FDIC got the property from a failed bank, because the borrowers didn't pay the mortgage. I closed on the property, became a property manager, bought a pair of bolt cutters, and started cutting the locks off the storage units that people didn't pay for. Suddenly ... I realized that I liked what I was doing for a living.

It was that day in October 1991 when my vision became clear: I wanted to buy (rather than build and develop) commercial real estate that was in disrepair and a distressed state at discount prices, improve those properties, and then use them as the platform to build my financial future. Reflecting on it now, I'm smiling. A huge weight was lifted off my shoulders on that day, because I'd finally found something to do that gave me purpose. Making money, having status, and being a lawyer in a nice (seemingly impressive) suit, was completely secondary to being passionate about what I was doing. I needed that passion to help me get out of bed in the morning, and suddenly I had it. That's when I began to heal. My self-esteem was improving. I had just now started to truly use all my God-given gifts, my education, my relationships and my drive: I finally had a focal point to direct my energy towards. I finally had intention.

Intention is the link between the philosophical and the actionable. It's the vision of what you want, where you want to go, and what it means for you to arrive there. I spent a lot of time as a young adult philosophizing about my place in the world; once I found my focal point, I had that purpose that I'd been looking for. This is what you need to strive to find in your quest for success. Some people find it easily and some have to struggle. Some suffer greatly and endure physical hardships, and for others it's emotional. Regardless of the hardships at hand, you have to find your vision. Identifying it is the first step towards success; it's the first piece in that martial arts move that allows you to dominate.

The risk of failing in pursuit of your passion is real, but it's a far cry from a life lived in dreary existence, without chance of euphoria. Many are unwilling to take that risk, but if you're looking for more in life, there's no way around finding that one thing that truly gets you going. Your intention is your passion, your purpose, and your goal. You need to do what it takes to live your life in the glory of passion.

ACCEPT THE EVOLUTION OF YOUR INTENTIONS

A goal is not always meant to be reached. It often serves simply as something to aim at.
   —Bruce Lee

A long time ago, I dreamt of being a master of the martial arts. I practiced constantly, pushing myself day after day. The discipline in my practice structured my life for twenty years, and I was happy for that to be the case. That particular goal, though, ultimately came to an end. A lifetime of rough activity like wrestling, gym hockey, and Jiu Jitsu left me with significant damage to my neck, and I was forced to give up the vision of myself as a grandmaster. I go to the gym almost every day now, and I love it, but it's not that original vision. The miraculous thing is that I'm still inspired and happy. I have new intentions to fill that void, and those passions keep me moving forward.

Pursuing your goals gives life so much meaning that the nature of the goal becomes immaterial. Siddhartha's life was not about obtaining Nirvana—it was about the path that he took. As a result of the experiences he had, he was finally able to reach Nirvana. As soon as he reached the goal, the story ended. Ambitious people never reach an ultimate goal, because as soon as they see the goal in sight, they adapt it. At first, your goal might be financial freedom. When you achieve financial freedom, your goal might shift to have freedom enough to travel the world. You might then decide to write a book or become an artist. If you stop having goals, if you stop chasing dreams, you take yourself out of the game of life.

> *We are changing, we have got to change,*
> *and we can no more help it*
> *than leaves can help going yellow*
> *and coming loose in autumn [...]*
> —D.H. Lawrence

You will go through different phases of your life, and your vision will change. That is inevitable. Besides death, the only certainty in life is change. Don't try to fight the fact that your vision is not what it once was. As much as you need to struggle to find your vision, you can't force it into being something that it's not. For me, physical challenges were what forced my vision to adapt, but visions can also shift for positive reasons. Learn to grow with your intentions; they are reflections of who you are. Be true to that.

INTENTION AND THE ART OF LIVING

The concept of being intentional is, in itself, quite a lofty goal. It's one thing to find intention for your career, but it's another thing entirely to be intentional about living your life on the whole. Try applying intention—passion, a vision, a goal—to everything you do. Be intentional about how you affect other people. Record that show, turn off the TV, and talk to your wife about her day or your upcoming weekend if your intention is to maintain a good relationship with her. Use Friday nights to start "game nights" with your family after dinner if your intention is to bond with your children. Volunteer your Sundays to picking up trash in your neighborhood if your intention is to improve the community. Do things you say you'll do if your intention is to be a great and respected member of society. Use your code of conduct, your focus, and your discipline to help you structure this. Everything you do requires intention. If you think about what you are doing deeply enough, all of the seemingly mundane activities can be tied to some lofty goal. If not, why do them? Being intentional to everything is a massive concept, and it requires a lot of discipline in order to maintain it. But in that pursuit, we find our salvation.

The Samurai warriors placed meaning and focus in every action, every breath. Their greater intention was to serve the nobility they fought for. That intention was behind sharpening their swords, crafting their arrows, and even sweeping the floors of their dojos. They found the ultimate holiness in service. The entire culture of the Samurai was focused on intention and making everything more important than the self, and that transcendence gave life in itself great meaning.

Possessing a clear intention is what will enable you to bring focus to your actions. Remember, the most important move of the process you're in is the one you're currently doing. As a Zen master once made clear: "When you make the rice, just make the rice." Be intentional about the use of focus for everything you do, and your actions will be transformed into something greater.

SELF-AWARENESS AND INTENTION

Watch your thoughts, for they become words.
Choose your words, for they become actions.
Understand your actions, for they become habits.
Study your habits, for they will become your character.
Develop your character, for it becomes your destiny.
—Unknown

One thing that has always appealed to me about the martial arts is that they are truly about growth. A master of the martial arts searches for answers for himself—and finds some!—through physical discipline, and those answers are ever changing. Because I have A.D.D., I found it difficult to study karate—it's honestly just hard for a person with A.D.D. to stand in line and practice repetitively, and in high school, it was the same story. I didn't have the same discipline and focus that I do now. I found it extremely difficult to sit down and study for hours like my peers; I was easily bored and had this constant nagging that I wanted to be doing something else.

In college, it was the same story; my studying habits were a little better, but not by much. I enrolled in political science, thinking the classes would keep me interested, but I came out with average grades. I went onto law school, turning page after page of the casebook, but it was the same. I had to start searching for answers in other ways—back then, I used wrestling as my outlet.

During all of this, a good friend named Anne introduced me to the novel *Illusions*, by Richard Bach. Though it's a novel, it deals tremendously with spirituality and the concept of reality, and Bach uses the vehicle of an adventure story to help the reader question his or her own reality. In reading it, I realized for the first time that I was on a deep quest for inner peace. It was an eye-opening moment, both because it helped me begin the long journey of defining my own intention, and because it bolstered my self-awareness in ways that I hadn't even thought about as a younger man.

In order to be intentional, you must be aware of your mental, spiritual, and physical self. There is no defining your goals if you don't have a grasp on who you are. That in itself is a quest, and an admirable one. The inscription in my copy of *Illusions* reads, "To a truly free-spirited person. Love, Anne." As a young man, I didn't know what that meant, but I swore I would figure it out. Years later, I have not stopped trying to understand what that means about me, and I owe Anne a debt of gratitude for guiding me in my quest to be self-aware.

In martial arts, if you re-distribute your weight, that one small adjustment will impact every move you make. You can't get to the point where you realize you need to shift your weight if you're not aware of your stance already. Explore and learn yourself so that you can make the adjustments needed to get to your ultimate goal. If you know you don't like making eye contact in conversations, but you want to be a personable businessman, be intentional about making that small adjustment. Try to make eye contact in every conversation you have, and the connection will be that much deeper. Self-understanding will feed into every intention you have.

Don't punish yourself when you screw up. We all make mistakes. Be aware of your issues. Acknowledge them, learn from them, and move on. As much as we might understand it and be able to weather it, life continues to come at us. This process is never-ending. It's a balancing act. Be intentional about self-awareness, and you can then be intentional about learning from your mistakes. Be ever-present. Be conscious.

BE PERSISTENT

Press on; nothing in the world can take the place of persistence.
Talent will not; nothing is more common than unsuccessful men with talent.
Genius will not; unrewarded genius is almost a proverb.
Education will not; the world is full of educated derelicts.
Persistence and determination alone are omnipotent.
　—Calvin Coolidge, Jr.

...nked the bar exam. Twice. I hated studying because I couldn't do it well. I didn't really want to be a lawyer, and I had to spend another six months studying, and then six more months, yet again, studying. I hated studying that material. But I fought on, because I sure as hell wasn't quitting.

Persistence is vital to success. I'm not proud of flunking the bar. It was humiliating and painful. I didn't do what it took to pass, and so I failed, and failed again. Ultimately, I passed, but it was only because I kept trying and did what it required to pass. That persistence served my intention at the time, and it also got me to where I am now. I wouldn't have bought that warehouse if I hadn't been at lunch with that friend of mine, and I wouldn't have known that being a lawyer was unfulfilling to me and that I needed something bigger, something better, if I hadn't pressed on.

I have a complicated relationship with my son, as many fathers do. I often get mad at him because I think he's trying to antagonize me (and he often antagonizes me because he thinks I'm trying to antagonize him!). We're both working constantly to improve our relationship, because we love each other, and our behaviors have heavily impacted the dynamic of our entire family. Even with our intentional effort, it's hard, and we do sometimes fail, but we have to keep trying or nothing will change.

Just recently, I yelled up the stairs for him to come down and see me. I must have called him about five times, and every time, I got absolutely no response from him. I started screaming at him, thinking he was being aggressive towards me—and it turned out that he was in the garage the whole time and never heard me to begin with. In order to accomplish my ultimate intention of improving our relationship, I have to be intentional about even the smallest of things—in this case, not making immediate assumptions or jumping to conclusions. And when I fail, as I did that day, I have to get up and try again.

Succumbing to failure is not an option. Neither is living without passion. The power of intention is strong, and if you harness it, you can get to where you need to be in life. Through focus and intent, you can make it. Be persistent.

✦✦✦

By embracing the power of intention, your ability to reach your goals will be greatly enhanced. Intention needs to be applied to everything you do. Practice being intentional. When you're tired, take a rest. Then practice more.

For many years, I was very focused on financial success, but then the economy blew up. For a while, I was really depressed; my goal suddenly felt unreachable, and I didn't know what to do with myself. One day, I was feeling so low that I started whining to my wife about the fact that nothing was happening with my business. My wife looked me in the eye and said, "It's not the economy that's holding you back. It's the fact that you're acting like a little pussy. You lost your swagger and you need to get back in the game."

She was right. As soon as a major challenge (like the bad recession we just experienced) showed up, I lost sight of my goal. I began to get caught up and focused on my mistakes and failures, and there were many. Negativity can be a very powerful, overwhelming feeling. I started to think about being intentional again, and then the light bulb turned on in my head. Not surprisingly, a few months later, I found a great real estate deal. By great, I mean in really bad shape … which equaled great for me! It was in horrible shape—leaky roofs, torn up kitchens and bathrooms, 25 percent empty! It was perfect—just what I was looking for.

I would never have found it had I not gotten re-energized with the power of intention. I went out, raised the capital, and closed on the deal. Years later, I'm now the proud owner of a beautifully renovated, 402-apartment building with only twelve vacancies. I'm happy, and I love doing what I do. Everybody falls off the wagon. Be intentional about finding your way back.

chapter 3

Commit to the Path of Discipline

The secret of success is constancy to purpose.
—Benjamin Disraeli

MY FRIEND HOWIE ONCE gave me a motivational letter defining success, written for life insurance salesmen in the 1920s. It reads, "Successful people are willing to sacrifice their comfort along the path to reach their goal. Unsuccessful people will sacrifice the goal to make the path more comfortable." Which are you?

If you want to be successful in any area of your life, it requires a commitment to the path—discipline—to get there. If you want to be a professor, you can't drop out of college. If you want to be a good husband, you can't screw around with girls. And if you want financial freedom, you can't piss away all your money on lifestyle, no matter how much you think you deserve it. The only way to get what you want is to be disciplined and focused while charging toward your goals.

Discipline, as defined by my martial arts teacher Michael, is "knowing what you want and doing something about it." Once again, it's the action that defines the larger concept here. You must be in accord with the goal every day. You must be in action to achieve the goal and always be committed to it. It's a form of self-respect. None of this works without perseverance.

The truth is that the meaningful satisfaction of life comes from the act of discipline itself. Goals are constantly evolving. Life is constantly changing. What you're disciplined about is secondary. The gardener, the baseball player, and the real estate mogul who are all single-mindedly pursuing their goals with passion and commitment all share in the satisfaction that emanates from their individual dedication. The goal doesn't matter as much as the pleasure of being in command of their destiny through their actions and focus. The way you respond to what life brings you will determine your success along the path. You must remain steadfast.

PRACTICE DOES NOT MAKE PERFECT

Practice makes permanent.
—Michael Andron

You may have heard the old adage, "Practice makes perfect." My teacher Michael always told me that that expression was incorrect; if you practice something wrong, it will never be perfect. What he said instead was a useful and important distinction: "Practice makes permanent." If you practice responding to something that happens in a specific way, it will become your natural response over time. That's what we are trying to accomplish here: to teach the development of techniques that allow us to be successful.

Understand that discipline is not just about practice. Practice is certainly a large component, but you must practice with your intent in mind at all times. That said, discipline extends past focused practice and training. It means you need to live your passion. It's the commitment. If your intent is to be a martial arts master, practicing every day is not enough. You have to train yourself to eat well so that you can physically carry out your moves. You have to understand the purpose of the moves and the intent behind each one. You have to learn about the history and the evolution of the art form.

The same goes if your intent is to be a successful business owner. It isn't enough to just run your business. You have to pay attention to the market and the demands of buyers; you have to go to networking events to expand your outreach; you have to budget and forecast for your year, so that come December, you aren't stuck in the mud.

Become an expert, but also remain a student of your subject matter. The learning should never stop. Be able to choose to devote time to your passion over something unnecessary. Train yourself to live your passion, so that you may live with passion while Walking The Way.

BECOME AN EXPERT

Discipline in learning ultimately yields opportunities, and, in the case of building a business, profit. We can't identify our opportunities if we don't understand them first. It has to do with our ability to be a vessel and receive what the world is offering us, and then apply it to our future. Medical specialists never fail to read the medical journals in their specific fields. It's a requirement. If they fail to do so, it can compromise their ability to move forward in their field. The same is true for all of us. If you want to be successful in anything, you have to first understand it. Identify your intention, and then help yourself become an expert in it. There are courses given in all fields. There are journals and periodicals. Find some path to learning your subject, and stay on it. I read our local newspaper; a daily real estate, banking and law journal; the local weekly business journal; *BusinessWeek*; and *The Economist*. I do this religiously. It keeps me up to date on all of the relevant details of my trade, both locally and globally, and if I know what's going on, I can often stay ahead of the curve.

Some colleagues of mine read *The Wall Street Journal*, *The New York Times*, *Barron's*, and *Forbes*. Find what's good for you, and do it without fail. When you find it, look for more. You can join social learning groups at a religious institution. You can audit college classes. You can join business groups that have lecture series. You can go to seminars. These are merely a few formal ways to grow.

Being disciplined about learning is not merely picking up the newspaper every morning and reading it cover to cover. Being disciplined means you are thorough, and you are always on the hunt. Find new ways to become an expert in your field. If your intention is to be a concert pianist, find new ways to practice that will expand your abilities. Visit concerts and master classes. Meet other concert pianists and talk to them. Always engage, and commit to it.

SUSPENDING GRATIFICATION

*Discipline is just choosing between what you want **now** and what you want **most**.*
—Unknown

We are not entitled to anything. We have to earn what we get, whether it is in relationships, education, or business. It's a common American story: hard-working immigrants sacrificed worldly desires for the family's future, only to have the second or third generation piss it all away over some misplaced entitlement issues. These ancestors of ours were suspending their immediate gratification for a bigger future for the next generation, and they were disciplined in its pursuit. What are your multiple goals? What might you have to sacrifice now to achieve the goals later? Remember, you will always have to pay a price to get what you want.

Until 2005, my wife and I diligently saved money, no matter how much we made. If you want to be a millionaire, you can't spend like a millionaire. We spent a lot less than what was coming in, we paid down our debt with the highest interest rate, and we tucked the rest away. In our early years, when we needed furniture, we found somebody who was getting rid of furniture. We allowed my in-laws to give us a bedroom set—I did not go out and buy a new one. We didn't take expensive vacations, and we drank water when we went out to dinner. When we visited New York, we stayed with friends instead of at expensive hotels.

We always were disciplined in saving, and that's why we were financially successful in the end. Pay yourself first, then pay your bills, and save the rest. When my wife and I were first married, our combined income was $40,000, and we managed to save $10,000 in that first year. Many of our friends would have spent it all, but in the end, we had money to invest. I could afford to buy a house and then sell that house for profit when the time came. We were ready to pursue our dreams when opportunities presented themselves, because we suspended our gratification.

A businessman who owns a small construction company and funds his pension to the maximum is suspending his gratification and diminishing his lifestyle so he can save for the future. The same is true for someone who pays an extra mortgage payment annually so that she can own her home sooner. In my case, my goal was to do this anywhere and everywhere that I could. I paid down debt. I invested in an IRA. I flipped the houses I was living in and bought commercial real estate, all at the same time. If I chose a higher standard of living, I wouldn't have had the capital to grow my future. Suspend your gratification and pay your future first.

Suspending gratification usually means you put yourself last. That said, the most important recipient for your suspended gratification is the future you, and you'll thank yourself later for your discipline. Think of it as being in two places at once. If you can consider your future self while making a decision for your present-day self, then you'll be able to stay the course.

I always point out to my children that people with expensive cars, fancy homes, and no money in the bank are examples of what not to be, but sacrifice doesn't always come in a tangible format. Picture a lawyer with lots of money in the bank. She's working in her chosen profession and loves it, but puts so much work in that she forgets to pay her own bills on time. Suddenly, she has bad credit, even though she's financially successful. The gratification that she has to suspend has nothing to do with fancy cars. She's got to sacrifice some time and energy so that she can pay her bills on time. She may not want to, because it's boring and she's not doing what she loves, but if her goal is truly to be financially successful, she has to pay the bills so that she doesn't destroy her credit and ruin her chances of investing in her future.

Sometimes, the price can be too high. Be careful in your assessment of these things. Sacrificing your ability to be a good parent and not being there for your children might be a price that is far too high to pay for financial success. Violating your moral standards, even in the grey areas, is a price that's too high for obtaining your goal. Always be within your code of conduct. There are things that are more important than certain success. What are they for you?

✦✦✦

The man who moved a mountain was the one who began carrying small stones.
—Chinese Proverb

I attended an entrepreneurial training school by the name of Strategic Coach. My coaches there always used the concept of "progress, not perfection." This mantra is so important because if you get close to your goal, but you don't attain it, you'll get frustrated. That frustration over not attaining your goal can lead to despair and another excuse to fall off The Way. Challenges will always come up: illness, death, relationship issues. All of these things are reasonable distractions, but you should not allow them to discourage you from picking yourself up and charging toward your goal. When you feel discouraged, take a moment and look back on your life, and see how much you've accomplished. You have made progress, and that is crucial. Think about the good things, take a deep breath, turn back around, and charge like a son of a bitch toward that goal. This is very hard to do, but it's significantly important. Focus on progress, and don't harp on the perfection. None of this works without commitment.

There is also the eighty-twenty rule. Many people don't start a project because they fear that they can't complete it perfectly. Try this: get 80 percent of the project done, and then complete 80 percent of the remaining 20 percent. You'll be surprised at how much you can accomplish without the fear of failure in your Way.

When you finally get into the discipline of obtaining your goal, you begin to see that the sacrifice you were making doesn't hurt at all. You'll see the benefits of the sacrifice begin to pay off, and from that moment, it's no longer a sacrifice and instead becomes a point of great satisfaction. Think about the smoker who decides to start running and getting into shape. Often, if they start enjoying the running, they will give up the smoking to enhance their running and can shake the addiction. What one person sees as a sacrifice, another sees as a way to satisfy themselves.

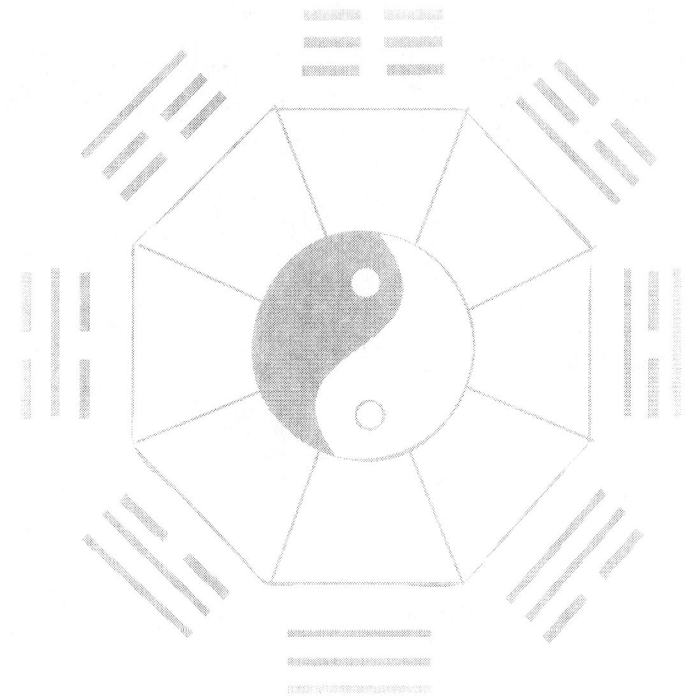

chapter 4

Focus and Self-Improvement

Whenever you want to achieve something, keep your eyes open, concentrate and make sure you know exactly what it is you want. No one can hit their target with their eyes closed.
—Paulo Coelho, *The Devil and Miss Prym*

A FRIEND OF MINE recently recommended a book to me called *What Got You Here Won't Get You There*, by Marshall Goldsmith. I bought the book and started reading it, and it was as painful as every one of those self-improvement books are, because I saw myself and my failings on each and every page. I couldn't read more than two or three pages a day, because it's hard to realize how much improvement you might need to do without getting discouraged. Somehow, though, by the end of the book, I knew that my anger and lack of control over it were compromising my ability to reach my goals.

In the past, I've allowed myself to react in anger in far too many situations: with my children, in the early years of my marriage, with employees who confound me. Goldsmith's book helped me realize that the expression of my anger was essentially the same as crying like a baby—I was allowing myself to get angry and letting it control me. I was allowing my weakness and my emotions to prevent me from making progress, simply because I felt like it. In short, I was violating every principle that I'd spent my whole life working on. It took me fifty-one years to see that my anger was holding me back in a huge way. I was sacrificing my goal for bad behavior on the path.

Despite the emotional difficulty it took to reach this epiphany, committing to improve this area of my life has made a remarkable difference. One of the techniques that Goldsmith suggests in his book is to announce to your family, friends, and colleagues that you will no longer react in anger. I decided that I'd use this technique to begin my newest goal of self-improvement.

One night, I sat my family down at the dinner table. "I've decided," I said, "that I am just not going to talk when I'm angry. I will not react in anger. I will take a day and think about something"—which is not in my character—"and ponder a reasonable reaction."

As soon as I made my announcement, my son licked his finger and stuck it in my ear. "I could make you break that promise in thirty seconds," he said, and everyone laughed. Graciously, no one in my family has thrown my promise in my face when I do react in anger, and I'm improving bit by bit.

I also had a meeting in my office, and I told all of my employees the same thing. They were more accepting of my "new leaf" than my family was. Every single employee of mine was greatly appreciative, and everyone liked working for my company much better after I'd made that effort. All it took were those words for me to become a better boss.

Since my commitment to thinking more before I speak in anger, I've been able to correct myself and improve my situations about 70 percent of the time. It's harder to correct at home than at the office, because I'm much more intentional at the office. At home I'm naturally more reactive, and the price I pay for screwing up is not immediate. Now that I've committed to the self-improvement, though, it has been a powerful thing for me. I've spent so much of my life improving myself already, and it took me fifty-one years to see that that behavior was messing me up constantly. My wife hated me, my kids thought I was crazy, and my employees thought I was out of control. I recognize now that my anger always stems from insecurity. When I'm not sure what to do with my kids, or my marriage, or my business, I get angry. Insecurity breeds fear. Fear brings anger. It is absolutely a death spiral. On the flip side, though, gratitude brings satisfaction, and satisfaction brings love. But I can't reach that flip side if I don't improve myself first.

Now that I'm in the process of improving this aspect of myself, I wonder how many more things there are like my anger that have gone unnoticed. And I wonder how many more benefits I'll receive in my life now that I have committed to being a better husband, or a better boss, or a better father. I try not to worry about how much money I could've made if I'd acknowledged my anger earlier. I try not to worry about my children possibly feeling better about themselves. I try not to worry about how my marriage could have benefited. I know now that my reactivity and anger was contrary to every positive force and goal of improvement I had.

I've since apologized to my wife and kids as well as some of my employees for that particular behavior. The truth is, I'm focused on looking forward, because I can't repair the past. I can only learn from it and then move forward the best I can. That's my idea of sticking with it.

✦✦✦

Intention and discipline are essential in your quest to succeed, but without careful focus, you'll fall short. Intention is your goal, focus involves the steps you need to take to get there, and discipline drives you through those steps toward your goal. Think of a dedicated martial arts student. His intention might be to become a grandmaster. He is disciplined in that he practices daily and studies hard. If he has no focus, though, his ability to succeed is hindered. The commitment of getting up and going to practice is useless if he's not paying attention. He won't learn stances and moves correctly, and his punches will be less powerful. Remember the man from Chapter 1 who spent his lifetime developing internal energy? If he puts that internal energy, that Chi, that *intention* behind everything he does, his punches have more impact. He wants to be a grandmaster; therefore, he practices diligently and works on developing his Chi. His ultimate goal is defined. Without focus, though, he can't achieve his ultimate goal because he can't hone the steps he needs to take to get there.

We also discussed varying levels of focus in Chapter 2. You can be focused on your ultimate intention, but you also must teach yourself to focus on the minutiae at hand that feed into your larger goal. Learn to take small steps, and you'll be at the top of the staircase, having climbed it to the best of your ability.

The World English Dictionary defines focus as "a point of convergence of light." As you learn to Walk The Way, find each one of those points that need to be treated with care. Sometimes the focus needed to achieve your intention is as simple as paying attention to your technique, and sometimes it's much larger. Focus requires a lot of brain-power, awareness, and discipline in practice. Don't get discouraged. When you mess up, brush yourself off and start again. Find ways to concentrate and invest yourself, and you'll be able to improve yourself with the goal of achieving success.

THE IMPORTANCE OF SELF-IMPROVEMENT

The will to win, the desire to succeed, the urge to reach your full potential …
these are the keys that will unlock the door to personal excellence.
—Eddie Robinson

One of the most important things you can do as you strive to achieve your goals is to focus on self-improvement. You can always, always be a better version of yourself, and that in itself is a commitment. Know that your goals would be irrelevant if you were the best you could possibly be; going after a goal involves climbing ever higher, and if you were perfect, you'd already have attained your goal!

In order to be successful in real estate, business, or life in general, you need to be committed to making your buildings, your business, and yourself as attractive as possible. When you improve yourself, you make yourself more attractive to the world, and you'll meet better clients, better investors, and make better friends. People will want to do business with you because of the way you live your life and the way you carry yourself. Wise-guys, liars, and poor businessmen have to constantly find new customers, investors, lenders, and friends. Successful, honest businessmen can be involved with the same people for years and compound their value. Be advised that value can range the gamut from love to monetary profit.

We've already talked about the benefits of being a life-long student, and we'll continue to touch on them in the chapters to follow. That's one of the first steps for your self-improvement—creating a base of knowledge to help boost you as you grow. The breadth of understanding of your field and related fields must continue to widen if you want to get to that lofty intention. As I said in the previous chapter, become an expert; and yet always remain a student.

Remain disciplined about your self-improvement as you

progress. Self-improvement is another commitm[...]
code of conduct and to your ultimate intention, a[...]
focus on it as you focus on any other step along The Way.

BE A LISTENER

When you talk, you repeat what you already know;
when you listen, you often learn something.
　　—Jared Sparks

As a person with A.D.H.D., I'm prone to movement. I change gears a lot, and it's hard to sit still. I could have avoided many difficult situations in the past if I'd been able to improve my ability to listen and focus. My relationship with my wife would be better. My children would have been less frustrated with me over the years. And if I'd learned sooner to keep my mouth shut in financial negotiations, I would have definitely have made a lot more money.

As I've grown, I always bear in mind something a friend of mine said to me when I commented on his success in life: "I wasn't always such a good listener." He's in his sixties now, and is highly respected by the community at large. His ability to listen is profound, and that statement has infused the way I handle scenarios with profundity, as well.

During the recession craze, I rented a large space to a young man at a very low rate, because rents were declining, and because I needed a tenant. In passing, he told his neighbor, another one of my tenants, how much rent he was paying. His neighbor, whose lease was written three years prior, was paying significantly more money for a comparable space. The next thing I knew, three or four tenants were clamoring for lower rent.

Despite the fact that they had leases with me, I understood their position, and I didn't want them to move out when their lease expired. I decided to meet with one of the tenants who were angry that their rent was too high, and I let him vent. It wasn't easy to get chewed out for fifteen minutes straight. I had to constantly remind myself to look him in the eye, and to focus on what was very important to him. My natural reaction was to just get out of there, but I managed to ask him, "What can I do for you?"

He was shockingly reasonable in his request of a rent reduction, probably because I'd taken the time to listen to him. I agreed to his request on the condition that he extend his lease an additional two years and sign a personal guarantee. He was so glad that I'd listened and agreed that he immediately accepted my conditions. If I had interrupted him and tried to force the issue, I might not have been able to accomplish this mutual resolution.

Lowering rental rates certainly means less profit, but now I have the benefit of an extended relationship in a time of economic distress. He personally committed to honor our agreement, and it turned out to be a win-win situation, even though I would have preferred to avoid it in the first place. There have been many times—in both my personal life and my entrepreneurial endeavors—where I completely failed to listen, and consequently wasn't able to reach a positive resolution. There have been so many times where I've jumped to conclusions with my children, and I was wrong.

By improving my ability to listen, I hope to minimize those mistakes in the future, and thus become more successful. It's a constant challenge for me, because it's one of those things that just doesn't come naturally to me, but it's an improvement that, if worked on, will penetrate every relationship I have.

> *Courage is what it takes to stand up and speak; courage is also what it takes to sit down and listen.*
> —Winston Churchill

One of the most challenging and rewarding parts of martial arts training is the fact that you have to respond to correction and criticism from your teacher by bowing and saying the word "Oos," or "Yes, Sensei." The same concept is found in the military—you say "Yes, sir," no matter what the higher officer has said to you. For many of us, keeping our mouths shut is difficult, but you could never succeed in a dojo or in the military without learning how to do it. When you can say "Yes, sir" without filling your mind with all the things you truly want to say, or resenting the fact that you can't say them, you're free. You can find clarity in that silence, and many learn this skill from meditation. Within that silence, you can visualize where you want to go and get there by a more direct route, as opposed to charging through the excess chatter in your mind. This is a lot easier said than done, but once again, great rewards come with overcoming great challenge.

Consider your own life. Are you a good listener? How can you bring focus to your exchanges so that you can improve?

The sad reality is, many of us learn how to do this only after having already paid the price for not doing it sooner. But life ain't easy. It's a struggle, and if you focus on improving yourself instead of focusing on what you screwed up in the past, you will find great personal satisfaction.

COMMUNICATE AND NEGOTIATE EFFECTIVELY

In my experience, I've found that listening is the single most important part of a negotiation. We've already discussed how that one simple step helped me—for most of my life, I had a hard time listening, but when I was busy talking, I didn't know what people wanted or how they felt. You can't help the other person if you don't know what they need from you. Negotiation is a two-way street, whether you're working on responsibilities in the home with your wife, or a big business deal. It can't be too lopsided, but if everyone can get what they want, then it's a win for both parties. Practice your listening skills with discipline—no matter how much you may want to interject, wait until you've heard as much as you can. Keep striving for improvement in this.

Every single conversation is specific to where you're standing and whom you're talking to. Find the right tactics to fit the context of your communications. In order to do this, you've got to be very aware of your own needs as well as the other person's. If it's a business negotiation, do some research. Find out who the other guy is and what his intention might be.

Be prepared. Make sure you're on top of your game so that you can handle the negotiation with focus. If I have an important meeting with a tenant, I always eat a meal before the meeting, so that I'm not cranky and hungry. I make sure my head is clear, and I create a list of things I want to accomplish that I can both review beforehand and bring to the meeting with me. I always know exactly why I'm there.

When a landlord is negotiating a renewal lease with a tenant, the tenant might only have one goal: to lower the rent. The landlord, though, has many goals. One is keeping the rent at a good rate for him. Another is lengthening the tenant's lease. Another is improving the contract. Another might be getting the tenant to not park his car where it doesn't belong, or getting him to pay that late fee he owes, or getting the tenant to pay the rent on time. There are always a million little issues to be looked at, and every one can be used in a negotiation, depending on what your priorities might be at the time. Widen that scope, and there's a good chance that you can give the tenant everything he wants, and you can get more for yourself in exchange.

Learn to be flexible. It's important to be conscious of all of your needs, but don't always try to make the last dollar or have the last word. You might get it this time around, but the next time, the person won't want to engage with you. You can give a tenant an ultimatum he doesn't like, and he might stay with you for the rest of the lease. But the next year, he'll have some time to prepare himself, and he might leave without even talking to you.

I've made that mistake before. Now, as long as I get within a comfortable range of my goal, I'm happy to take the deal. I don't always try to get the most possible if I don't have to. I try to get as much as I can while still maintaining a positive relationship with my customer. I'm not an expert on negotiation, but I am a practitioner. I've negotiated thousands of leases and deals, and I've worked with my wife every day through a relationship and through raising children. Learn from your experiences.

Communicating effectively does involve a large amount of self-awareness, and that's another massive area of self-improvement. You can't get much from other people if you don't identify yourself as much as you can. Practice taking inventory on yourself. What do you need from other people? What are your goals for interactions? Do you know how to listen? Work diligently on self-awareness, and you'll be able to improve on all facets of communication.

EMULATE YOUR HEROES

Unconsciously we all have a standard by which we measure other men, and if we examine closely we find that this standard is a very simple one, and is this: we admire them, we envy them, for great qualities we ourselves lack.
—Mark Twain

Each one of us has different goals, agendas, and priorities. Focus and commitment to self-improvement is a way to stay constantly in a mode of growth. One technique for constantly self-improving is to find others with specific qualities we respect, and emulate them.

My brother David, who is very introspective and takes the time to think before he acts, has, on occasion, regretted not acting immediately in what might be a time-sensitive situation. Recently, he told me that in some of those scenarios, he asks himself, "WWBJD?" I asked him what it meant, and he replied, "What Would Ben J. Do?" As my brother, he knows exactly what I would do, and in asking himself that, he gives himself the opportunity to click right into my mindset if the situation merits it.

We don't have the luxury of acting exactly the way we feel all the time. Signing a deal without consulting your business partner, or approaching your boss with a raise request right before a major deadline—these are just some examples of acting without thinking, or acting in the wrong situations. Even in simple situations, thinking before acting is crucial. Sometimes, when my wife doesn't understand something I've said, I have to curb my impulse to snap back in disbelief that she doesn't get it. It's one thing to respond with "I love you very much, but you're not understanding this," versus "What are you, a freaking moron?" She's just trying to get through her day—there's no need for me to take my immediate frustration out on her.

Sometimes, acting impulsively will destroy relationships and opportunities. It can have a negative impact on our lives, and so we must emulate the behavior of someone who we know would handle it better. Applying their wisdom and techniques is a great strategy.

Author Stephen Covey suggests imagining your own board of directors. You put them at a table in your mind, and when you have an issue, you can access their opinions.

This way, you can have at hand the advice and wisdom of Martin Luther King, Jr., or your grandfather, or a particular colleague you admire. Fill your table with people you deeply respect, and in time, with lots of practice, you can tap into their behaviors and create more options for yourself that you might not consider on your own.

When I was seventeen, I spent a year in Israel. At the time, my father was ill, and so I went to buy him a gift in the hopes that he'd be cheered by it. I found two prayer shawls that I thought he might like—one was basic and went for seventy-five dollars, and one was absolutely gorgeous, for two hundred dollars. I bought him the less expensive one. He passed away three years later, and I inherited the prayer shawl. Every time I put it on, I feel like a cheap jerk, because in hindsight, I know I should have bought him the beautiful one. My nature at the time was only to be conservative in spending my money. My brother Michael was generous, almost to a fault. Now when I'm in a similar position, I ask, "WWMD?"—What Would Michael Do?—and I get over myself, and spend the extra money. Accessing Michael's behavior makes spending the money easy for me, because I understand and appreciate how his generosity touched me in the past.

In business, we can do the same thing. Ultimately, we're able to keep these behaviors that we want to have for ourselves. What works for you? Adapt to the effective tactics, and if they don't work, throw them out and find other ones. Different people find different things that move them. Constantly search for techniques or practices that you can add to your arsenal.

BE WILLING TO TAKE RISKS

Never was anything great achieved without danger.
—Niccolo Machiavelli

One of the most difficult aspects of self-improvement, and life in general, is opening yourself up to take risks. It's terrifying to put yourself out on the line, but if you want improvement—*change*—it's absolutely necessary. If you're attacking life in any way, if you're on those quests, then life will call on you to step out no matter what you do.

I take hundreds of risks every day, and many of the times that I do, I'm scared to death. Even something as simple as a tenant wanting to get out of his lease early is a risk. If I let him out of his lease early, I'm never sure that I can rent his space out to someone else for more money, let alone get enough from someone else to break even. I'm working on a deal now, and I'm really hoping to get it, but I know that as soon as I sign that contract I'll be terrified—maybe I didn't value it right, maybe the market won't continue to move in my favor. If I want to keep on my quest, though, I have to sign that contract and take that risk.

My son Sarya attended university in Israel for a year after high school. One day, he called my wife, Dorit, and I and let us know that he wanted to join the Israeli Defense Forces. I was so proud of him for his bravery, but I was terrified. I had to balance my philosophical ideals and what I believed was good for him with my fear of his death, and it was unbeliev-ably challenging.

As difficult as that risk was for me, it was harder for Dorit. She had the final say over whether Sarya would join, and she let him go with the promise that he'd come home at the end of his tour of duty. I think it was maybe the hardest thing she'd ever done in her life, and I am so proud of her for opening herself up to that potential danger so that Sarya could go on his own quest.

Sarya went on to serve in the paratroopers in division 890. He served with distinction, and at the end of his tour, they offered him to stay on and take the sniper course. Sarya graciously turned them down, and he came home like he promised he would.

When Sarya walked through that door, it was the first time in my life that I felt pride. I thought I'd felt it before, but I'd never been overwhelmed with it like I was then. My son had chosen to face great challenge, and he came back a better man for it.

Of course, now that it's months later, Dorit and I keep hearing horror stories that he never wanted us to find out about while he was over there. There was a time when Sarya was stationed on the Lebanese border, and he and his unit were getting shot at regularly. They were not allowed to return fire because it would have started a major international incident, so they all just withstood the shots and hoped for the best.

I freaked out when he told me this. "What did you do?" I asked in disbelief.

Sarya shrugged. "I ducked."

My other son, Azi, has shown exceptional bravery in the face of risk as well. When he was eleven, he started suffering frequent and intense headaches. For a year and a half, _ after doctor told us it wasn't a big deal, until finally one of them sent Azi in to have a CAT scan.

It turned out that Azi had a Chiari malformation, which is when the cerebellum sits lower in the skull than it usually does. We saw a neurologist, who assured us that typically, this kind of thing wasn't a problem, but that we should have an MRI done just to be safe. We took his advice and went for the MRI.

When the neurologist looked at the results of the MRI, his face went absolutely white.

"What is it?" I asked.

"We need to perform surgery right away," the doctor said. What the doctor saw on the scan was that Azi's skull was causing pressure on his cerebellum and pressing down on his spinal column, preventing his cerebrospinal fluid from flowing properly.

All of a sudden, Dorit and I were in deep despair. We did tons of research on the situation, trying to figure out our best options for giving our twelve-year-old major brain surgery, and we finally decided to go to Miami Children's Hospital in Florida. We shared everything we knew of Azi's situation with him; we felt that to hide anything from him would be wrong. I'll never forget Azi's face as he was wheeled into the operating room. Simply put, he was brave. Dorit and I held onto that courage as we sat in the waiting room, wondering how young Azi could be so much stronger than we felt.

Fortunately, everything went smoothly. The surgeon finished the procedure an hour early and came out to tell us that Azi would be just fine. My son woke up from the surgery in the Pediatric ICU, looked at us, and he said, "Is it over?"

"Yes," I said, tearing up.

"Is it fixed?" he asked.

"Yes."

Azi looked at me from that hospital bed and yelled—as only a kid could—"I'm never having surgery again!" I knew in that moment that I had my boy back.

The boy in the Pediatric ICU bed next to us was sixteen. He'd had a brain aneurysm while playing soccer, and he was never coming back. And there I was, having Shabbat dinner with my own child in the ICU, and we knew we were going to be okay.

The risk of that surgery was tremendous, but the risk of not doing anything was even greater. As terrifying as it was to send my son into that operating room, I know it was even more frightening for him. We made the choice we had to make, despite the fear and the danger, and Azi was unbelievably courageous throughout all of it.

With Azi, we didn't have much of a choice but to take that chance on surgery. Sarya's situation was more of a choice, and yet each of my sons came out better men for having taken those risks. Risk is equivalent to danger, but if you want be successful, you have to push the envelope. You have to step outside of your comfort zone and do the thing you are afraid to do if there's a reasonable chance that you'll come out better for it.

Be smart about taking your risks. Jump right in, because

you can't succeed without doing so, but do some analysis first. If you want to purchase an old building, make sure that it's not going to cost you millions more to fix it than you're likely to make on it. Don't go out sailing when there's a 95 percent chance of a hurricane. There are possibilities in everything, but you have to be reasonable about looking for them. Find your balance in each situation, and then take the risks you need to take in order to fulfill your quest.

KNOW WHEN TO SAY NO

A challenging aspect of self-improvement is learning how to say no. It takes a lot of practice. If you say no all the time and are completely intransigent, then you'll be rightfully perceived as inflexible, and your relationships will be difficult to maintain. People will not want to engage with you in any way unless they need you for something. But if you don't know how to say no, you'll get taken advantage of, and it will be harder to progress. Learn to say no to your kids, to favors you can't afford, to discounts you feel obligated to give.

What's often harder is learning to say no to yourself. This is another form of discipline: hold yourself accountable and don't give in to yourself. Say no to that extra piece of chocolate cake, or to sleeping late instead of going to exercise. Say no to tempting but morally deficient opportunities. Make those sacrifices.

In the world of non-institutional real estate, if you always waive late fees, none of your tenants will pay rent on time, and you'll end up in an unfortunate position. Say no. Collect the late fees, and in doing so, you'll earn respect. I don't like to demand my rents or late fees from my tenants, but sometimes I have to.

Recently, I was with a tenant who'd only been in my building for about four months, and he had yet to pay his rent on time. I had to think hard about how to approach him. I didn't want to establish myself as the bad guy, but I didn't want to throw myself under the bus either. Finally, I called him into my office.

"Listen," I said. "Every time I see you, I say hi, because I like you, but we have a problem since you haven't paid your rent on time once. I've got three proposals for you, and you can pick any one you want."

"Okay," he said tentatively.

"One," I said, "you can start paying on time so that you have no late fee, and I will appreciate you as my tenant. Two: you can pay late every month, and actually pay the 10 percent late fee when you do it. I'll like you better as a tenant because you're paying me extra for the space and I'll be able to afford a new wing on my house. Or three: You can leave at the end of this month, and I will sue you for the money you owe me.

"I don't want to fight with you, and I really want you to like me, but I'm not going to beg you for the money that you legally owe me according to our lease. So here's a one-time offer: If you give me the rent that you owe me, plus half of the late fees that you owe me, I'll wipe the ledger clean and we'll start over. And in the future, if you pay me late, you'll give me the late fee too."

He sat there dumbfounded, and then got his checkbook out and started scribbling.

Despite the recession and despite his tough times, I ultimately felt I had to go to him in this manner. I wasn't being particularly nice, but I cut him enough of a break that he could both respect me and pay me. I was straightforward, and straightforwardness can go a long way in developing a mutual and productive understanding. You don't always have to be nice. You can say no, and you should when it's appropriate.

You also need to be able to say no when it comes to an opportunity where you know you cannot deliver. Earlier, we talked about being self-aware, and this is one of those instances where it's absolutely imperative that you know yourself and know your limits. Saying yes to anything can get you into all kinds of trouble, and it will ultimately harm your reputation if you fail.

Once I was chosen to be a secretary for an organization. In hindsight, I have no idea why I agreed to do it. I have A.D.H.D.—I can't remember what I ate for lunch, let alone be comprehensive memory for a large organization. I had to find a solution, and so I delegated. I asked one of the other board members if I could write a check for a donation in exchange for her keeping the minutes of the meetings for me. She agreed. I wanted to be on the executive committee, because that's where all the decision-making happens, so I found a way to delegate what I couldn't do and still meet my obligation.

I'm certainly someone who says, "Let's jump in," but those risks should always be calculated, before completely committing. I spend a lot of time analyzing options and weighing outcomes. Not walking away when I needed to has hurt me badly. Sometimes, it comes in the form of me agreeing to do a task I'm unqualified to do, and sometimes, it only comes as one extra obligation that I can't afford to add to my plate at that time. Check your skills, your availability, and yourself before you agree to things.

BE KIND

Just like your mother, you're unfailingly kind—a trait people never fail to undervalue, I'm afraid.
—Albus Dumbledore
(from *Harry Potter and the Half-Blood Prince* [film])

We've discussed many reasons why kindness is so easily repaid in life, but I think Professor Dumbledore of *Harry Potter* fame sums it up best. There are grand people, great wizards and even greater mystical creatures in their world, but somehow, the energy emitted from a truly kind person generates the greatest power of all.

Find ways to be well-liked, but do it from the goodness of your heart. If your kindness isn't genuine, it's not going to benefit you or anyone else you encounter. Find ways to be nice. I don't have to upgrade my tenants' spaces, but on occasion, I do it because I want to, and they appreciate me for it.

One summer day, I went with my daughter Ariana to the beach. By chance, we ran into someone who happened to know the daughter of a friend of mine. I spoke very highly of my friend to his daughter's friend, and they ended up doing business together. At the meeting in which they signed the contract, his daughter's friend told my friend that the real reason he engaged with him was because of the way I spoke about him. Now, my friend loves me even more, because I helped him without even trying to. I didn't speak well of him to make him money, either—I did it because I cared about him and I meant it. These people knew they could trust my friend; he got some business; it was a win-win all around; and it was all because I took a few minutes to speak kindly about a person that deserved it.

Be friendly every chance you get. Say hello, strike up a conversation, talk to everyone you can. I'm attracted to intelligent, ambitious people, and I'm constantly seeking out these people in every field. When I find them, I talk with them, and if I like them, I ask them to go to lunch. I find a way to help them, introduce them to someone in their industry, help get them a job with someone and access their network. If the feeling is mutual, you have the opportunity to be introduced to a new idea, a new book, or a new business opportunity. Find a way to give them something of value. Being friendly and nice will provide you with all kinds of opportunities that those who avoid engaging don't have. It's hard to be kind all the time, but find a way. You don't know how things will come back around to you, but they will. The kindness will always come back to you.

APPLY THE THINGS YOU LEARN

We can consciously use the relationships we create to make our lives better in many ways. We can use the techniques of listening to better improve our relationships or our negotiation skills. We can constantly use the quest for wisdom and knowledge for personal satisfaction. The reasons we should do these things will always change, but the importance of doing it always remains the same.

Applying what you learn as you go is an essential component of self-improvement. If you read a book on efficiency in business, but you're unable to apply anything that you learned to your practice, then you miss out on most of the value from that learning. If you understand interest rates and mathematics, but you don't apply it to the cost of your own borrowing, you miss out on the benefits of your knowledge. Apply it.

Throughout history, there has always been the discussion of the importance of wisdom versus that of knowledge. I was stuck in one of those challenges. I had a line of credit with the bank at 5 percent. I have a small loan on a property at 6.25 percent. The easy answer is to use a small portion of the line of credit to pay off the loan, and that way I'll save 1.25 percent. If you're purely math-based, then the answer is easy: pay off the loan. However, I'm thinking about buying more real estate, and I might need that portion of my line of credit in the future. I didn't know what to do—I felt stupid paying the unnecessary interest on the loan, but it's hard to borrow money, and I didn't want to risk minimizing my future.

Personally, I came to a conclusion. I decided to pay extra today for opportunities tomorrow. I'm not going to pay off the loan, but the value of assets to the additional capital might be significantly more. When I was younger, I would have come to the exact opposite conclusion, and at that time, it might have been the right answer for me. But now, I'm using my wisdom (analysis of the market) to override my knowledge (the mathematical equation above). It's a risk, but it's appropriate for the given scenario. As you learn to apply all of these techniques, learn, too, to weigh wisdom versus and knowledge, because there isn't always an easy answer.

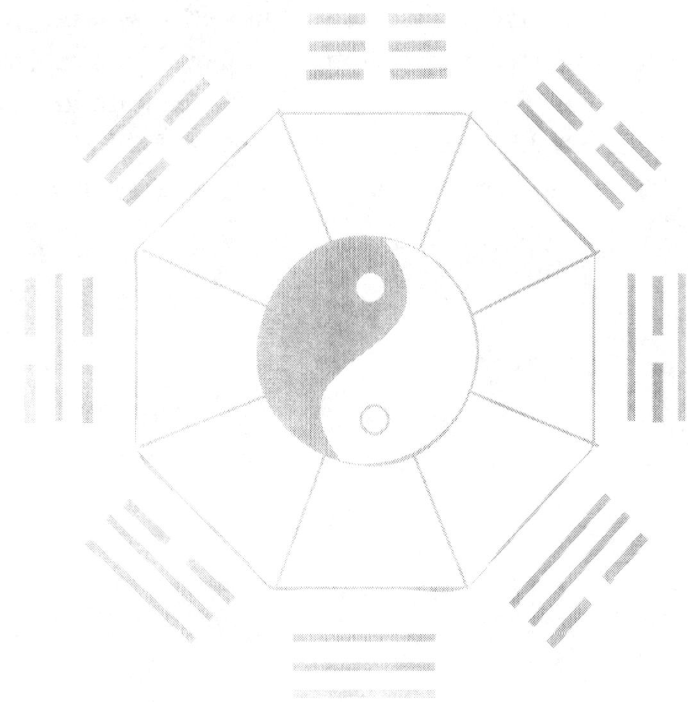

chapter 5

Develop and Maintain Your Code of Conduct

And what is that ancient path, that ancient road, traveled by the Rightly Self-awakened Ones of former times? Just this noble eightfold path: right view, right aspiration, right speech, right action, right livelihood, right effort, right mindfulness, right concentration ...
—Nagara Sutta

IN 1988, I PURCHASED a twelve-unit building. My building manager, a woman named Chris, was a tenant there. We quickly settled into a great rhythm: Chris got half-priced rent for managing the building, and I paid her by the hour for extra maintenance work that she did around the property. Chris was one of the most genuine, fine and upstanding people I'd ever met. We were from two completely different demographics—she was low-income with a small amount of education—and through my relationship with her, I learned that quality and integrity don't discriminate.

After I'd owned her building for about ten years and worked with Chris throughout that whole decade, I swore to her that I'd never sell the property without her permission. This was my promise to her, and an example of how I chose to live and respect my idea of proper conduct, and morale.

Years after that, the building skyrocketed in value, and I was dying to sell it. I mentioned the idea to Chris, and she said worriedly, "Not yet—I need a couple years. Please don't sell it yet." She'd spent years helping me and giving of herself, and the least I could do was grant that request. I'd given her my word. Even though I wanted badly to sell, I stood by my code of conduct and held onto the building.

Three years later, Chris told me to sell. I looked at property values, and I was thrilled to find that the building was worth even more than it had been when I'd originally wanted to sell it. I just knew that God had shined his light on me and granted me good fortune because I'd done the right thing earlier and kept my word to Chris. I sold right away, and rolled the money I made through a 1031 tax-free exchange into another property.

It was a disaster. It was one of the most expensive deals I'd ever made. During six of the first eight years that I owned it, the new building didn't bring in any profit at all. I was positive that God was laughing at me because I'd immediately thrown all of my money into this next deal, looking for more money. And just as suddenly, eight years after I'd purchased it, it started to do well. Go figure.

In hindsight, I find the entire scenario incredibly amusing. The surprise in all of it is that it's not about God blessing us or punishing us. It's about doing the right thing. Chris treated me kindly and with honor, and in return, I treated her kindly. It's about a lifetime of acting with integrity and love. Ultimately, things will work out or not, the way they always do. And you do the best you can.

✦✦✦

CREATING A CODE OF CONDUCT

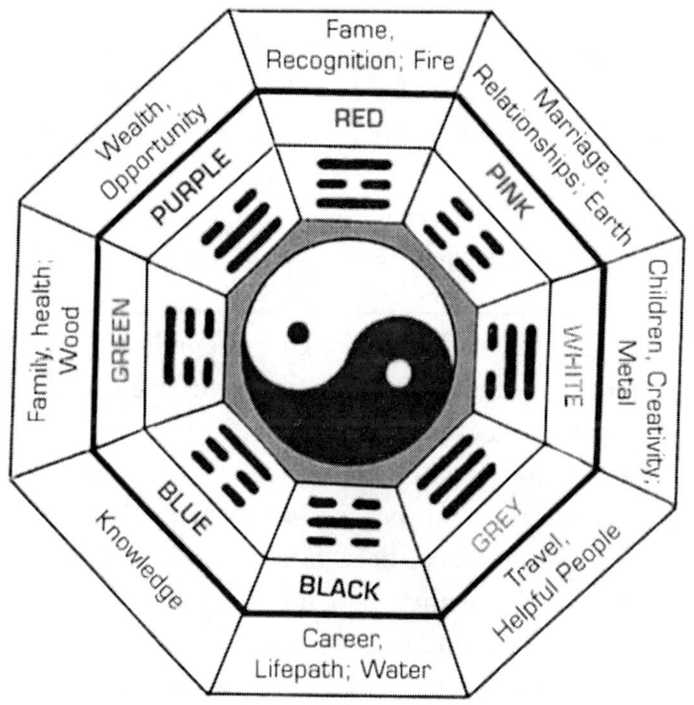

Above: the bagua, used in Taoist cosmology to represent the eight fundamental principles of reality

The Noble Eightfold Path is one of the principle teachings of Buddhism. Through walking that Noble Eightfold Path, one can cease their suffering and achieve self-awakening. Think of it as a kind of code of conduct for Buddhism: right view, right aspiration, right speech, right action, right livelihood, right effort, right mindfulness, right concentration. Wisdom, intention, ethical behavior, discipline, focus—these components are all present in the Jumper's Success Formula, but the commitment needs to be made to live by that code.

Standards are certainly subjective, but the basic principles of morality remain the same in virtually every culture: live with love, practice kindness, exude integrity. We each have personal reasons for arriving at our codes of conduct; our experiences and knowledge define who we are, and we—consciously or unconsciously—make choices based on things that we know.

Take the time to define your code of conduct and to find the intention behind it. It can be easier to live by a certain structure if it's more tangible to you. What are characteristics that are important to you? Are there any spiritual laws or commandments that you find particularly poignant? Find out what you consider to be right and wrong, and be intentional about living within those moral constraints.

Be intentional, too, about the "borders" surrounding your code of conduct. If an ethical line is hazy, it's easier to cross it. Is a white lie against your code of conduct? If it isn't, find where a white lie becomes an outright lie and then stay away from that point. Stick to those terms with discipline, and don't compromise them—that way, you can be completely true to yourself.

"Thou shalt love thy neighbor as thyself." Why? Because every human being has a root in the Unity, and to reject the minutest part of the Unity is to reject it all.
—Baal Shem Tov

Once you've developed your code of conduct, consider actions that will further define it. When you live by your code of conduct, you demonstrate who you are to others, and you can also make clear your expectations for their relationships with you. We've talked extensively about being kind—find ways to be kind, and be genuine about it. Practice it. Kindness will certainly allow success to come more easily to you, but you'll also feel better, and people around you will too.

Your code of conduct goes beyond selecting specific characteristics and behaviors that are important to you; it permeates everything you do. Use it with your wife and kids. Use it in your business. Use it for others—but use it for you, too.

The following sections are designed to help you in your quest for a code of conduct, but they're not absolute rules. Like the other practices in this book, these are things that have helped me in the past. Feel free to use what works for you, but also know that your code of conduct is unique to you and to your own experiences, and it's up to you to find out for yourself what constitutes acceptable behavior.

INVEST IN CHARITY

No one has ever become poor by giving.
—Anne Frank

As we will discuss further in Chapter 6, there is a learning advantage that volunteering can give us: it exposes us to new perspectives, new people, and new values. Being generous can be a great component of your code of conduct, for, as we've said, if you give, then you receive tenfold.

Find ways to keep on giving. It comes in many forms. Buy your father that more expensive gift—it might help him understand your appreciation for him, and it will also help you to grow a deeper appreciation for yourself. Teach a young person your martial arts skills. Be emotionally supportive of your friends.

One of the many ways to give is to invest in charities and non-profit organizations. You can donate time, money, or both, and the results you get will astound you. I currently sit on the board of my kids' school, the board of a large, local philanthropic organization, an educational program for special-needs children, and an international board that helps victims of terror. In the past, I also was on the board of my synagogue and the board of my city's planning and zoning committee. I go to a lot of charity dinners. I'm active and involved in the world. Having a full life like this results in lots of friends and contacts, but it also brings deep personal satisfaction and spiritual growth. Give back to the world that has given to you.

Earlier, we referred to your code of conduct as your reputation. If you give of yourself, people simply will appreciate you more. They'll respect you for your societal involvement, and they'll find great pleasure in helping you to succeed when the time comes. You'll make more money or meet more girls, and in my case, you might get referred to potential investors or tenants. There is also no better place to find like-minded investors for whatever goal you might be working on.

I've often heard people say, "Nobody asked me to be on the board. How do I get involved?" More often than not, you have to walk yourself into that dojo. Be proactive. Get on a committee and volunteer. Do it two or three times, and you'll get noticed. It's unsurprising that hardworking and generous people always get invited to participate. Write a check, show up, and work hard, and in just a few short years, you might be sitting on a board of directors.

BASE YOUR RELATIONSHIPS ON INTEGRITY

To be trusted is a greater compliment than to be loved.
—George MacDonald

I once had a contract on a building with a friend of one of my very close business associates—a great opportunity that had been brought to me through networking. Legally, I was able to squeeze the guy for more money in the contract, so I went ahead and did it. Though I was within my legal contractual rights, the guy trusted me, his friend's friend, and didn't think I would risk a genuine relationship for $300,000. He went through with the sale, but afterwards, he never wanted to do business with me again. I did not break the laws of morality, nor did I break the laws of the government—but I didn't live up to a standard of integrity that I should have.

On some level, I actually enjoyed the lost business opportunities that resulted from this exchange. Most times in life, we don't get to see direct results of our behavior, but as I watched him trying to sell properties, avoiding my offers in the process, I could immediately see karma coming back around. I'd sacrificed a trustworthy relationship for extra money, and as a result, I didn't get more money later down the road.

Be intentional about being genuinely honest. Sometimes that means sacrificing immediate gratification or having difficult conversations, but it's worth it. Don't go for the extra cash from a friend just because you can. Tell that prospective tenant about your policies from the get-go. Be open about your feelings with your girlfriend.

You must also be honest with yourself, and that self-acknowledgment will feed directly into your ability to be honest with others. If you have a personal issue, don't be afraid to find out what's at the root of it. Use that honesty and awareness to feed your intention.

ENHANCE AND DEVELOP YOUR EXISTING RELATIONSHIPS

Take care to always enhance the components that are already working well for you. It simply makes good sense to keep customers or girlfriends happy. Once I've got tenants in my buildings, I want them to renew their leases, so I focus on caring for them and ensuring that they are content. I regularly upgrade their spaces with things like new lighting and carpeting to make them more comfortable, and I acknowledge when they've been good customers to me. This is usually done when they are renewing their lease for multiple years. Not only do I feel good about being honest and good-natured, but it's also a great investment for the future. I've had tenants who thought I was difficult and left, only to come back later when they realized how honestly I run my business. They told me that they'd rather deal with a difficult but honest person than an easy-going guy who's a liar. That's "earned loyalty," and it separates you out in the marketplace.

Not every relationship is successful. Sometimes people don't like me, so I do my best to spend the least amount of time on those relationships. I do get along with many people, though, and I'm always looking for ways to create more value for them. This way, I can retain good clients, get more deals, and get invited to much better barbecues.

Creating value in relationships like this is giving of yourself, and it should come from the goodness of your heart. That having been said, receiving benefit is a natural by-product of such kindness. A graduate student who does research for the professor always gets the benefit of that work in their grades, because they learn from the research and can apply it to their own work. This entire give-and-receive concept makes the world a better place, and it keeps your own environment enjoyable.

Sometimes, these actions are wasted. We never know if we're dealing with a "taker"—someone who does nothing for you except drain you of your efforts. When you do discover that someone you're dealing with is a "taker," just stop giving so much and keep it on a strictly business level. That way, you'll be able to carry on business with them for an extended amount of time, and you won't be emotionally drained by wasted effort.

This will sometimes include firing a very competent but negative employee, as difficult as it may be. When I started attending my entrepreneurial school, the Strategic Coach, I told my class that I had an employee who fit that competent-but-negative bill. At least three people advised me that a negative employee, no matter how profitable, would destroy my future. They were right. I was scared, but I got her out, and my business is a much more comfortable environment for me, for my customers, and for my employees. The freedom I garnered from it was invigorating, and the energy I was using to fend off her negative attitudes could be put to many more positive pursuits. She went on to take a job that she was much better suited for, and so her life was enhanced as well.

❧❧❧

Those who stand for nothing fall for anything.
—Alexander Hamilton

My message here is important—it is imperative that you maintain your code of conduct. Figure out what's important to you and set that standard. Never stray from it. Remember that it's okay to say no to things (really!). If you know you don't have the funds yet to donate thousands to charity, or you won't perform your best, or give something your all, you are not doing anybody any favors by half-assing it. Take baby steps: donate a small amount that is reasonable; offer your help on a different project; put your efforts towards something you *know* you can knock out of the park.

Without integrity, without the commitment to do good and be good, it's easy to fade into the crowd of schmucks who only care about making money, or showcasing their "status." If you can harness your own code and abide by it, you'll stand out from the crowd as a solid, trustworthy businessman, partner, or friend. You'll like yourself better. And yes, you will get invited to better barbecues.

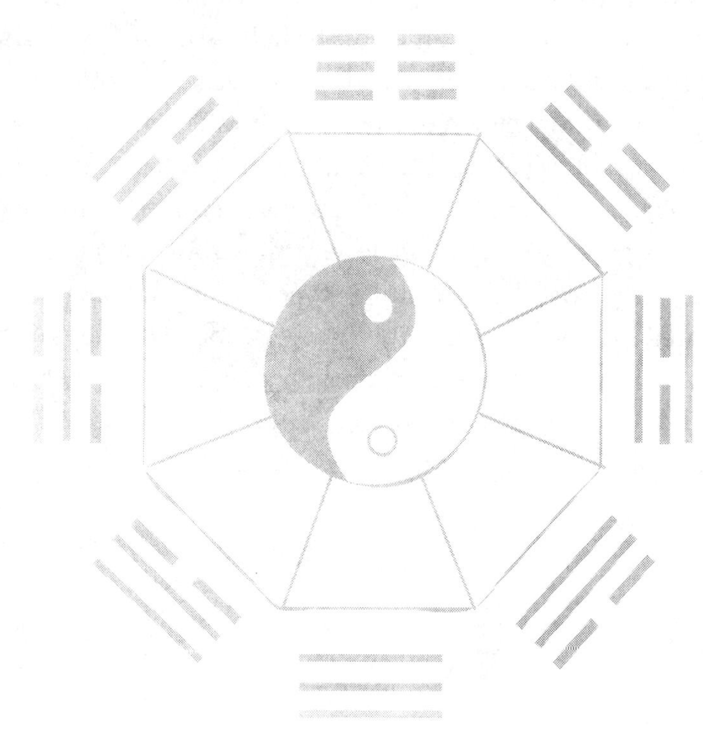

chapter 6

Engage in Life-Long Learning

Live as if you were to die tomorrow. Learn as if you were to live forever.
—Mahatma Gandhi

EARLY ON IN MY marriage, my wife, Dorit, who is a great singer, was in a musical. On the morning of one of her performances, she'd told me to fill up the car with gas, but of course, I didn't bother. That night, she performed beautifully in the show, but on the way home, we ran out of gas right in front of a closed gas station. It was about eleven o'clock at night, and we were in a neighborhood that I didn't recognize—and to make matters worse, we had no way of contacting anyone for help since we couldn't afford a cell phone at the time. They had just come out and were very expensive. The gas station we were in front of must have been out of business, because there were no lights anywhere except for one street light that gave us just enough light to know that it was really, really dark out.

Needless to say, Dorit was chewing me out for not getting gas earlier, and what made it worse was that I knew she was right. Moreover, I was starting to get nervous about being stranded there. Twenty minutes after we ran out of gas, a broken-down, late model Pinto pulled up, driven by an elderly, straggly-looking man. It looked like life had been hard on him, and he didn't speak any English at all.

He parked and got out, and asked us in Spanish, "*Puedo ayudarse?*"—can I help you? I told him in my broken Spanish that we needed gas. He nodded and smiled and pulled away, and I just knew I was screwed. I had absolutely no confidence in a good outcome.

Twenty long minutes later, we could hear the same car grumbling down the street toward us. To my surprise, the elderly gentleman got out of the car with two half-gallon milk containers filled with gas. I was so grateful that I folded up a fifty-dollar bill to give him. I was by no means rich at this time in my life, but the guy was clearly poor, and I wanted to express my appreciation with something that would help him. He looked at me, smiled, and said, "*La haces para un otra persona*,"—you do this for someone else. He refused to take my money, and went on his merry way.

I will never forget that man. I learned two very valuable lessons that day. One is that a small act of kindness can change somebody's perspective forever. This man became one of my great teachers, and he was only in my life for a fleeting moment. The other lesson is this: money is not the answer to everything, but emotional content is. This man, who clearly needed fifty dollars and probably couldn't afford to buy the gas he'd just bought for me, didn't want to diminish his act of kindness by receiving money. For him, it was about giving, and nothing else.

I had no intention of learning anything that day. My only goal was to get us home before my wife killed me for not listening to her. As I write this, though, I'm filled to the brim with emotional gratitude, and I look forward to repaying this act of kindness many times over in my life. I meditate on his gift, and that helps me energize myself.

Why is it that if you tell a small child not to touch the hot pot on the stove, they will invariably keep going back to it? As soon as they burn their fingers on the pot, they get the message. Sometimes, we can teach ourselves to get the message without having to get burned. That being said, some of the greatest lessons of my life came from mistakes I made. I touched a lot of pots.

My karate teacher, Michael, would always correct my stance in practices. He told me, "If you can correct this one little thing, the impact it will have on your ability will be significant, because you use this stance in all of your martial arts practices." If we realize that every bit of learning that we do could affect every area of our lives, how excited would we be about doing it?

I'm going to use the term "learning" so as to not differentiate between great wisdom, specific financial analysis, or any other cerebral input that arguably have nothing to do with each other. We need to make it all ours. We need to suck in learning like a sponge in water. Our nature and personality will direct us toward the type of learning that's best for us, but our mind must keep us focused on remaining disciplined about it.

*Understanding is the one-dimensional comprehension of
the intellect. It leads to knowledge.
Realization is three-dimensional—a simultaneous
comprehension of head, heart, and instinct. It comes only
from direct experience.*
—Dan Millman

Learning opportunities always exist. Our ability to receive that learning, coupled with the mentality that we'll use it in our future, needs our constant attention and work. Learning happens when we're open to it, but if we are intentional about receiving it and disciplined and focused in pursuing it, then the world is full of opportunities for us. Getting a formal education in school is important and valid, but often, as a result of not having been out in the world, our ability to absorb our learning there is limited. I went to law school immediately after I finished my undergraduate degree, but I was so ignorant that I didn't appreciate the opportunity. I ignored information constantly because I had no clue that I'd have any need for it in my life, and I wasted a great opportunity because I wasn't willing to receive what was offered.

These days, when you get into Harvard for undergraduate work, they suggest that you take a year off to work or travel, and start to gather new experiences. When you want to get your MBA from a top university, they prefer for you to have a few years of work experience under your belt for the very same reason. Somehow, we must find a way to put ourselves in a position such that we will learn from what is around us.

BE DISCIPLINED

Whatever it is that you are interested in learning about, be disciplined in its pursuit. In Chapter 3, we discussed becoming an expert; understand that it is imperative that you commit to your learning and to your chosen subject. Life-long learning means picking up pieces of a giant puzzle. Over time, the pieces will begin to come together, and gradually, whole sections of that puzzle will start to make sense. For committed life-long learners, the puzzle is never completed—it just keeps expanding.

GET EMOTIONALLY INVOLVED

Intent is an essential part of everything; in particular, our ability to absorb something ethereal like learning. We don't know how or if we will apply this learning to our future needs, so the emotional importance we place on our quest for learning is crucial. Without it, what impetus do we have for this pursuit? If you want to be a doctor and you're in medical school, you understand why you're there. But if you're in the world and you want to find love, make money, and be involved in your community, your family, and other events, how, then, do we apply the quest for knowledge to those goals? Without emotional involvement, learning will get boring very fast, and your gain will be significantly diminished.

In the beginning of Bruce Lee's movie, *Enter the Dragon*, he is pictured teaching a young student how to throw a side-kick. During their interaction, he smacks the kid on the top of his head and says, "Emotional content." What Lee's character was trying to teach the student was that any act with emotional drive behind it will be much more potent.

Whether we're learning how to kick someone, or learning how to learn ourselves, we must apply this concept diligently.

When I was in law school, I was just trying to get through. My only goal was to have fun, and then graduate. In the lecture hall with me were many thirty- to forty-year-old newly divorced mothers whose passion and intensity to learn the information was far beyond where I was at the time. They wanted to be lawyers. They needed to be self-sufficient because they had to support themselves and their children. They were intently focused, and I was just messing around. What they got out of law school was much more than anything I was able to receive. It's the same principle with immigrants who come to this country and are willing to do anything to survive, versus a spoiled middle-class kid who is just worried about his comfort along the way.

My daughter Ariana once was cast in the musical *Joseph and the Amazing Technicolor Dreamcoat*. She decided that in order to be her best at her role, she would improve her ability to sing. I had no idea that through training and practice you can get better at singing, but my wife did. They spent a lot of time together discussing the nuances of breath and how to use it to produce different sounds. From my perspective, it was simply wonderful to see a mother and daughter together, working passionately at something they loved, and I was deeply proud of my daughter for committing to and succeeding in improving her skills. The results were more than just a stellar performance in her show—they included a deepening level of emotional connection between two people. The emotional content for my daughter allowed her to learn, but it also assisted her in strengthening her relationship with her mother.

There is certainly learning that we must do for our education or businesses that repels us. Accounting, for example, has always bored me to tears. Once I analyze the numbers for my own company, though, and they're put together in a way that I understand, I find it fascinating and enlightening. Adding the emotional content makes the work palatable for me. When they're my numbers, it's not about accounting—it's about my business, and it interests me.

How, then, do I get emotionally motivated when I have no personal stakes involved? The answer is easier said than done, but it is simple: I try to stay connected to my ultimate intention. I'm a board member of a large philanthropic organization, and part of my duties include reviewing the budget. Reading those numbers is like sticking a needle in my eye, but if I want to be a good participant, I need to understand them. If I can remind myself of my larger goal—in this case, being a member of this board that I truly admire and care about—then I can push through those tedious tasks. Keep emotionally connected to your goal, and if that connection is strong enough, it can serve as your motivation. If it's not in accordance with any of your intentions, then why do it? That's where the Jumper's Success Formula comes directly into play. You need to be focused, disciplined, and intentional; and in this particular case (supporting a charity of my choosing), aligned with your personal code of conduct.

When people start in business school, a basic requirement is for them to read *The Wall Street Journal* every day. If you truly don't care about what you're reading, you will get a lot less out of it. If you realize that there is great power in what you will gain by reading it every day for ten years, then your focus will improve. You'll truly care about understanding the material in front of you. Your desire to re-read paragraphs you don't understand will override your frustration, and the joy you will receive by gaining more understanding will be enhanced.

Be emotionally invested in what you want to learn, and in finding new things to learn. It must be considered a holy quest for those that are pursuing constant improvement. Often, this pursuit will lead you down paths you never thought you'd walk, and open doors you never knew existed.

We all want different things out of life. We're all traveling in different directions. If we do not limit our ability to receive what's around us, if we train ourselves to open our eyes and hearts and souls to taking in and processing everything we can, then our individual goals will be much brighter and more meaningful.

BE OPEN TO NEW VEHICLES FOR LEARNING

Realize that everything connects to everything else.
—Leonardo da Vinci

Having a broad view of learning means you're always open to new paths of discovery, which will open new doors in your life. I mentioned earlier that reading Richard Bach's *Illusions* was a moving and powerful experience for me. It was happenstance that I even read the book; it was a gift from a friend. Because I was open to new concepts, the book revealed to me a quest to be more free-spirited and less caught up in my insecurities. Thirty years later, I'm still working on that quest. I wasn't intentional about learning until Richard Bach woke me up. Through my commitment to that quest, and through my interest in *Illusions*, I started reading Hermann Hesse. Then I started reading Ayn Rand. *Illusions* was the precursor to all of my martial arts training, and to my love of Eastern philosophy. From there, I started learning about Chinese art from a cousin of mine. Now, when I look at Chinese calligraphy, I think about Siddhartha, and I find it calming. That one little path, out of the thousands in my life, turned out to be deeply meaningful and life-changing. All of our paths continue into infinity, and once you realize that that's where you're headed, you'll be more open to them.

My brother David is a periodontist. He went to Harvard for dental school, and from there, Columbia for periodontics—he knows how to study. One day, many years ago, he decided that in order to be even more successful in his profession, he would do well to learn more about business. He chased this goal with discipline. He read voraciously and took courses in many different areas of business. Years later, I find his business advice very practical and enlightening. It comes to me from a place that's far from my entrepreneurial perspective, because the base of his knowledge is in a different field. Don't underestimate the power of new perspectives to assist you in your learning.

David's quest for a broad base of knowledge outside of his chosen profession has many positive outcomes, and they would have never happened without his pursuit of self-education. Now we have a new depth in our relationship that comes from the shared understanding of similar business interests. Combined with our complete and total filial trust, this deeper level has been financially beneficial to both of us.

What's more important: the forest or the trees? I would suggest that they are equally important, but they need to be studied and engaged in completely disparate manners. We must learn different things in different ways. The financial aspect of real estate has almost nothing in common with the physical management of the properties, but you can't always do one without the other successfully. Never narrow your focus too much without simultaneously looking in a different direction. *Everything is somehow intertwined.*

SURROUND YOURSELF WITH TEACHERS

I've had many teachers throughout my life, and they have each taught me many things. This, frankly, is one of the greatest gifts I've ever received. I had teachers who taught me about God and philosophy and history. I had friends that taught me about loyalty and betrayal. I learned that I could be good or bad. My brother Michael taught me how to look a girl in the eye and smile. Not only did that one tip work well with women—it proved, too, to be a crucial skill in all relationship development. Through his example, he also showed me how someone can get by giving; he loved nothing more than the act of giving. My brother Sandy taught me that if I didn't work hard and focus, I would turn out to be a bum—but that if I did use discipline and focus, I would find satisfaction. Two brothers and their lessons; so different, yet integral to my growth.

In high school, I was sent away to boarding school, and I never really felt comfortable there. I spent a lot of time at my cousins' home, trying to settle down. Alan and Miriam, my cousins, opened their home to me and treated me as their own. I listened to beautiful classical music, heard Miriam diligently practice piano, watched their family devour books, and heard them discuss art at the kitchen table. It was drastically different from the world I came from, and its impact on me was powerful. They taught me how to appreciate much more of what life offers, and they taught me to love and give. I owe them so much, and without that childhood experience, I would never be where I am today.

I met the aforementioned Professor Sober in ninth grade, but because of my A.D.H.D., I was unable to study karate at a young age. I admired him from afar, and I listened to his stories. Years later, while studying meditation with him, I realized that I had found a teacher for life. Though I see him rarely at this point in my life, his impact on me is profound and ever-present. I eventually was able to spend a year studying karate with him. And when I moved to Florida for law school, I studied under his senior student Michael for the next eight or nine years.

Whereas Professor Sober was a great warrior, Michael was a great healer. He was not a teacher that I would have picked for myself, but he became one of the great ones in my life. Sometimes our relationship was strained, but I believe that as a result of that struggle, I got even more out of our relationship. Call on those different perspectives. Seeing the world differently than someone else doesn't mean that they can't have a profound effect on your life—in fact, differences sometimes lead to greater gain.

I've had many teachers that influenced my developing years—including my brilliant Jiu Jitsu teachers, Professor Arturo Morera and Dr. Philip Chenique—and I'm so grateful to them. I've continued to surround myself with those that I find highly intelligent, generous, and kind. There has always been a mentor around when I needed one. I rarely perform an act of kindness for someone else without thinking of those that did them for me. My gratitude toward them is eternal. Be intentional about finding mentors for yourself. And, equally important, when the opportunity arises, be a mentor for others.

I can't conclude this topic without talking about my father-in-law, David. When I first started buying real estate, my understanding of it was very minimal, and my appreciation for the properties themselves was non-existent. Over the course of time, David taught me that if I treated the real estate with love, it would reciprocate—but if I tried to use a Band-Aid and fix issues improperly, the result would be poor. David showed me, with great patience, the connection between the real estate and the tenant who occupies the space, and it was a lesson that was monumentally integral to succeeding in the business. If your tenants are physically comfortable and have confidence that you will take care of the property, they will then be able to stay there for an extended period of time. Then, and only then, can you begin to think about making money—which is where I wanted to be.

David was always there for me, and he always went out of his way to help me to understand things. Our visions were never the same, but it led us to better dialogue, better challenges, and through that, better understanding, and deep love and respect for one another.

When you meet the great teachers of your life, you very well may not recognize them for who they are, and that's okay. Sometimes the greatest lessons are learned further down the road. As you assess the things you want to improve, consider those who do those things well, and find out what they have to say. Anybody and everybody has something to teach you, if you are willing to accept their experiences and knowledge.

READ BOOKS

People can be wonderful teachers, but the books you read and the understanding that you glean from them is what prepares you to be ready for the people you're going to meet. Sharing opinions on books with others is a great means of breaking through all sorts of barriers, and it can help you begin honest dialogues. Often, people have defense systems or proverbial walls around them, and finding comfortable common ground, like a book, can lower their defenses and lead to more meaningful exchanges.

Don't hesitate to read many different types of books. You'll find that great wisdom is applicable to drastically different topics. My earliest understanding of economics came from Ayn Rand's *Atlas Shrugged*. It helped form my earliest fiscal and political views, though I read it a long time before I had to think about making a living.

The Luck Factor, by Brian Tracy, put into words so many concepts that I thought about and didn't know how to express. The basic premise of Tracy's book is that we create our own luck. One thing leads to another, and if you're aware of that and actively pursue positive results from current action, your entire life will change. The most powerful thing I got from literature was the vocabulary to express my own opinions. Acquiring the vocabulary to say what you think in a communicative manner is a significant and powerful skill—practice this diligently.

Take advantage of the Internet as well. If you don't have time for a book, find an article or two to read. And if you don't want to read books, listen to them! Technology now offers us *many* choices. Your ability to uncover significant wisdom and knowledge is at your fingertips. Revel in it and make it yours.

DON'T BE AFRAID TO TALK TO STRANGERS

I had a business associate who once told me that when he travels, he always flies first class. I knew he wasn't making all that much money, so I asked him why. He told me, "You never know who you're going to sit next to in first class." It's true—an opportunity could be sitting right next to you. Chat with people you don't know, and find out what they have to offer.

Don't be shy. Ask people about themselves, and you'll find out quickly if they want to interact with you or not. If they don't want to, there's nothing lost, but if they do, it's an opportunity for both of you. I was on a flight once to Utah, and I sat next to an eighteen-year-old, and I mentioned that

I love skiing. It turned out that he loved it too, and knew of this mountain ski resort called Snow Basin. I decided to take a trip out there, and it was wonderful. It surprised me that I had anything in common with an eighteen-year-old on college break, but I would never have found the beautiful mountain resort without his help—it's a prized skiing locale, but only by people who live in the area.

At a board meeting once in 2008, I found myself sitting next to a stockbroker named Ken. He and I got to talking, and I told him I didn't understand why the stock market kept going up when the economy was doing so poorly.

"I should probably just dump all my stock," I said offhandedly.

Ken looked me in the eye and said with meaning, "If that's how you feel, it sounds like a good idea."

The next day, I sold all my stock. Two weeks later, the market crashed. I know I was lucky, but I would never have had the confidence to do it if I hadn't talked with him that day. Soon after that, I ended up opening an account with him, and I now have three times the amount that I originally had in the stock market. Not only that, but Ken has become a friend. We both benefited from that fortuitous conversation.

Everybody has something to teach you. You can meet people who have suffered and struggled and lived and overcome. You can learn from people who grew up rich, and from people who grew up poor. Listen to people's stories, and share experiences. There's so much value in exchange and interaction, and the ultimate by-product could be a deep and meaningful relationship that rises from the place that you least expect.

I joined Entrepreneurs' Organization (EO), a global business network, many years ago. I was there for over five years, and learned a tremendous amount from the people in my forum. A dozen strangers, sworn to secrecy, sharing and trying to improve their lives through the help of each other. I still have friends from EO, and I look back on that time fondly. I'm also a member of Vistage, a widely known CEO group, and I have gained more than I imagined just from staying involved. Strangers are opportunities. Keep your mind open to them, and if you give, you'll receive.

VOLUNTEER AND PARTICIPATE

Giving connects two people, the giver and the receiver.
This connection gives birth to a new sense of belonging
[...]
—Deepak Chopra

Volunteering your time and participating in activities you might not usually do can open you up to worlds of learning. There will be conversations you never considered at certain meetings, and problem-solving strategies that you never knew existed. Try volunteering at a homeless shelter, and then working at a black-tie event. Be as expansive as you can in your participation—it will broaden your worldview in profound ways. Be intent in your learning, and be open to new directions.

For two summers, when I was fifteen and sixteen, I worked at a summer camp for special needs children. I had a ton of fun, and I made a lot of friends there, but there was one boy in my bunk who was never happy. His name was David. He was autistic, and he had severe scoliosis. The only time I ever saw him happy was when the whole camp was singing. During those group sing-alongs, he was transformed. His whole persona changed from one of discomfort and pain to one of euphoria.

One day, I was sitting in my bunk, fifteen years old with no experience and no training, and David started punching himself in the face repeatedly. I didn't know what to do. I was terrified. Finally, I grabbed him to stop him from hurting himself, and he resisted me so aggressively that he hurt my hand.

"Ouch," I said, rubbing my hand. He looked at me and suddenly stopped his violent frenzy.

"Ouch," he said, and rubbed his hand too.

Somehow, we shared a moment, the understanding of pain, and his attack on himself ceased. From then on, when he got hostile with himself, I would say, "Ouch," and rub my hand next to him without physically engaging him, and he would always come around.

Those two summers influenced me greatly. I remember one incident on the second day of camp during my first summer there we had a water fight. A boy with cerebral palsy named Cliff was in a wheelchair, and he wanted to participate in the water fight too. Cliff asked me and my co-counselor, Alan, to get him some water. Alan told him to get his own water, and I thought he was being a jerk by not helping. Two weeks later, Cliff was flying out of his wheelchair, crawling on his hands and knees, to fill a cup of water for a water fight on his own. Needless to say, by the time he got anywhere with the water, it was all over him, but I finally realized what Alan had been doing for Cliff. By not helping him or allowing me to do so, he was being helpful rather than mean. At home, Cliff never left his chair, never bloodied his knees in the pursuit of pure joy. It was Alan's wisdom and experience that led him to make one simple choice, and that choice greatly improved the quality of Cliff's camp experience.

OVERCOME FEAR OF IGNORANCE

If I had allowed my lack of knowledge of real estate to stop me from buying properties, I don't know where I would be today. When I was trying to practice law, I always wanted to be the client, so I eventually bought and sold twelve foreclosed houses with no real idea of what I was doing. I hired people to fix the houses, I showed them to anyone interested in buying them, and I sold them—and eight of the twelve brought in good profit. Over the course of time, I learned more and more. I pursued knowledge of real estate in every way that I could while experiencing it on a daily basis. Sometimes, you just have to jump. Don't be afraid—just find A Way to make sure that you're not landing on the rocks.

✦✦✦

Be diligent, focused, and intentional in the pursuit of knowledge. It's up to you to seek it out, and to absorb it in any way that you can. Always remember that from experience comes great knowledge. Engage yourself.

chapter 7

See Obstacles as Blessings

*Each problem has hidden in it an opportunity so
powerful that it literally dwarfs the problem.
The greatest success stories were created by people who
recognized a problem and turned it into an opportunity.*
—Joseph Sugarman

OBSTACLES, THOUGH FRUSTRATING AT best, are inevitable. One of the many techniques that will help you in your dojo is to harness your challenges and turn them into opportunities. Use that self-awareness that you've developed to help you pinpoint obstacles. Don't discriminate in dealing with them—some come from external sources, and some don't. Identify them, and try thinking about them differently. How can you turn an obstacle into an advantage for yourself?

My A.D.D., for example, could easily get in my way (and has often!) and become a major obstacle, or I could use it to my advantage. My challenge is to see it as a gift and use its inherent qualities to my distinct benefit. I call it my "genetic A.D.D.vantage." In many ways, it helps me blow away the competition.

Part of having A.D.D. means that I'm constantly in motion, and I often forget what I was thinking about from one minute to the next. Because of this, dealing with issues immediately works best for me; if I don't deal with them right away, they'll be lost. The advantage here is that because I delegate so many of those issues quickly, I can get more done than other people who work much harder.

Despite the fact that I've become very proficient at tackling issues immediately, I still sometimes worry—especially if I can't deal with them right away—that I've forgotten something important. One solution I've discovered is to leave messages on my assistant's voicemail, day and night. It ensures that the issues will then be analyzed, or put on my calendar, or simply remain present until they're taken care of. Knowing that my assistant will get my messages in the morning and make sure I review them gets rid of that stressful, unproductive, black cloud of worry hanging over my head at four in the morning.

My fear of forgetting details has inspired another opportunity: I maintain a detailed calendar. The calendar on my Blackberry is linked to my office calendar, and everyone who works for me can see it, comment on it, or add to it. I certainly have boundaries to protect my control of it, but the open calendar helps both me and my staff to be efficient with time and communication. My wife also has access to the calendar, and she can add relevant children's appointments and personal dates as well.

I use my A.D.D. to my advantage. What are your issues? What causes anxiety and lack of clarity in your thinking process? See if you can identify your personal obstacles, and then turn them around to help you.

OBSTACLES IN BUSINESS

Recessions are definitely financial obstacles, but they are also the best times to buy businesses and real estate. Now, if your current business is suffering, it's very hard to get the confidence to find another one. Many businesses fail for reasons that are fixable. Real estate deals go broke because of financial issues that have nothing to do with the underlying real estate. If you can look past the existing problems and see the opportunities, though, you might be able to jump on one. This is the definition of seeing obstacles as opportunities. If it were easy, everybody would do it.

The opportunity here lies in converting an obstacle into a powerful tool to help you accomplish more than you could before. We must always strive to make ourselves more efficient with our time, minimize our anxiety, and maximize our clarity. If we accomplish these goals, we will have more freedom … and freedom is good. These same rules apply if you're a college professor or managing a construction crew, but the structure of your business needs to be based on your own unique needs. When you understand obstacles are blessings in disguise, problems will be diminished. Did I mention that freedom is really good? That's worth working toward.

PRESENT AWARENESS

*Do not dwell in the past, do not dream of the future,
concentrate the mind on the present moment.*
   —Buddha

In Aikido (a Japanese martial art), as in life, you can use the energy of your opponent to your advantage. A pivotal concept in Aikido is to step out of the way of an attack while simultaneously putting yourself in a position to dominate your opponent. In order to do that effectively, you have to be completely in the moment—totally present. How you respond to the attacker after that is secondary. If we learn to respond to difficulties while we are in a centered and controlled place, the danger will be minimized, and therefore, we will be much more effective in our response.

Instead of dwelling on your shortcomings or overwhelming yourself with problems, look for the opportunities and look beyond the dangers. Of course, we have to analyze the dangers and find ways to overcome them or step around them. Your goal, however, is to be calm in the face of adversity. If you don't want adversity and obstacles, then you can't be in business for yourself. Everyone who is engaged in the market will get sued, buy a bad deal, or end up with an irate customer. There is no way to avoid problems if you are engaged. You're forced to deal with them. Why not make them better?

As much as we need to prepare for issues, we simply will not always be prepared. But if you train yourself and remain aware and centered, then at some point in dealing with an obstacle, opportunities will arise. You will be able to approach them from a much more strategic and ultimately more powerful place. This concept applies to all areas of life, and we must practice this relentlessly.

Just like the Aikido master who, when attacked, somehow winds up behind his opponent and in control, you must anticipate, act, and remain in control. In life, there will always be attacks of one nature or another. Someone will quit, someone will become ill, someone will die, someone won't love you as much as you love them. Focus on seeing a positive result, even in a painful situation. Even though the reality of your present cannot be avoided, know that your intent and state of mind can and will impact the inevitable future.

Obstacles can indeed be opportunities to practice the self-awareness that you've been developing. The important thing to understand is that you need to prepare for these issues before they happen, so that you can anticipate them more fully. Practice on smaller issues, and as the skill grows, you can apply it to the larger obstacles. You must be intentional in training yourself to look down on your issues.

There is no "three strikes and you're out" rule. You're allowed to become emotionally caught up and make mistakes. You might not be able to prevent making mistakes, but you must be able to become aware of the moment. Always strive for self-improvement, so that the pitfalls in your future will not only happen less, but be less overpowering than those in your past.

WHEN YOU CAN'T STEP OUT OF THE WAY

If the winds of Fortune are temporarily blowing against you, remember [...]
A kite rises against the wind—not with it!
    —Napoleon Hill

A few years ago, I was mixed up in a loan with bad people. I did nothing wrong, but since I was the only one who was collectible, I ended up getting sued. The bad guys insulated and protected themselves in a hundred ways, but because I'm honest and have some money, I'm the target. Hopefully, when all is said and done, I'll win the lawsuit, but it will—at best—cost me $30,000 in legal fees, take a year of my life, and cause pain on a personal level.

I cannot step out of the way of this blow. It might cost me a lot of money, time, and energy, and the frustration and anger I feel is a big distraction from my life and ultimate intentions. How do I deal with this danger and see it as an opportunity? Well, for starters, I'm going to fight like a son of a bitch. I'm going to defend myself with every available legal means, and I'm going to tell my wife it'll be okay, even if I'm not sure. I'm going to try to look at every obstacle in the way of resolving this problem and try to deal with each one. Simultaneously, I am going to continue to charge toward my goal. The key, though, is my emotional state. I have to control myself and keep my mind clear. Without clarity, the ability to function in the face of the stress and frustration would not be possible, and clarity is not easy to accomplish.

Controlling my anger in this particular issue has been difficult. The person suing me knows me and doesn't care how it affects me. I had nothing to do with his loss. As infuriated as I am, though, I know that my anger won't help me. It will cloud my judgment and stop me from moving forward.

Now, I understand that my legal troubles are unique, to myself and my business, and that I am fortunate enough to be able to protect myself and use the resources I have available. These kinds of things don't happen to everyone, and if they do, not everybody is able to hire a legal team. However, my message here is not that I have legal woes, but rather that despite this nasty snag, I am using it to learn—to learn to control my anger, to learn to remain positive, to learn to see clearly, and to learn to not get caught up in situations like this again. This can be applied to any daily situation: from getting a speeding ticket, to having your computer break down in the middle of a project, to invoicing clients.

Don't let your obstacles control you. Instead of surrendering to your emotions and bemoaning the issue with self-pity, be self-aware and engaged in the present so that you can minimize your unavoidable dangers. Even if you do fail to step out of the way of the attack, you still can correct yourself, find your center, and move forward. Mistakes happen, and none of us are perfect. Sometimes awareness comes from that lonely, miserable spot that we find ourselves in after we've been emotionally smacked upside the head. As long as we are conscious enough of where we are, we can be conscious enough to regain our center, silence our demons, and press forward.

Ultimately, your objective should be to look at your situation from above, with a little emotional distance. If you can do that, your potential is infinite. If you can handle your issues from a centered, calm, and distanced perspective you will find the best way to deal with them. But if you allow the obstacles to overcome and consume you, they encroach on all of the other opportunities in your life. Acknowledge the problem and seek out the best help you can to resolve it. Look at overcoming each separate obstacle to solve the problem, always keeping your intention in mind.

DEALING WITH INSECURITY

Most of the important things in the world have been accomplished by people who have kept on trying when there seemed to be no hope at all.
—Dale Carnegie

One of the most trying obstacles that I deal with on a daily basis is my own insecurity. I do not like feeling like a failure, and I want people to like me. The biggest mistake I made when I was younger was worrying about not knowing what to do as a husband or a parent. I've paid the price for those behaviors my whole life.

It takes a tremendously strong warrior to fight insecurity when it rears its ugly head. Our negativity and our insecurity are the most dangerous, debilitating, and egotistical expressions possible. It is the most selfish expression of yourself, to be so scared as to allow your insecurities to control you. If you feed your **insecurities**, they get hungrier. If you starve them, they'll be satisfied.

Insecurity is the flip side of the ego, and if you let it get to you, it can destroy your life. Fighting it is an ongoing battle, but a necessary one. A basic principle of Eastern philosophy and meditation is to let those feelings pass through you. Take those feelings and put them in a bubble, and then meditate on that bubble just floating away like a big balloon, disappearing into the sky.

I'm not a psychologist. I'm not an expert on this. I've never been able to fully defeat these evil spirits of the ego. But when I can control them, good comes. The only chance we have at success is in dealing with those feelings.

Humans are filled with animal instincts: desires and emotions and issues they got from their parents, their gene pool, or from society. Our job is to get up every day and battle that. We battle it in many ways. To me, the best way to battle it is to be the best, most successful person you can be. Fighting the good fight, being charitable, helping your friends, being smart, making money, being engaged in the world—all these things allow us to fill our consciousness with positivity.

CONTROL YOUR MIND

As he thinks in his heart, so he is.
—Jewish proverb

We must control our mindset. It's critical. You must be intentional with how you feel. The difficulties will still exist, so being positive doesn't necessary mean being delusional. If you focus on your opportunities and keep your attitude positive and your mind focused though, you can get more done. If you focus on the positive, there will be no room for the negative, and it will help keep your mind clear and calm. In my case, my consciousness is full and active at all times—my mind never shuts down. I need to be positive at all times and aware of my consciousness, or my mind obsesses with problems.

Professor Sober taught me that the difference between a black belt and a brown belt was that a black belt could put his entire emotional essence into focus to execute a technique at will. The brown belt could execute the same physical technique, but without the focus or the intention, it would be inferior. The brown belt cannot at all times access his complete emotional being into the technique as the black belt can, at will. Emotional content, as Bruce Lee said, is critical.

My teacher, Michael, taught me karate and energy work. As I mentioned in Chapter 3, he defined discipline as "knowing what you want and doing something about it." Your mindset is critical; focusing your intent to see obstacles as opportunities is a skill that can be learned. It doesn't mean there isn't a problem to overcome. But by realizing there is an opportunity hidden behind a danger, your anxiety will be diminished, and your clarity of vision and thought will be enhanced.

There is no one rule that applies to everybody, but I have some ideas. For one thing, if we are truly grateful, there will be no room for negativity in our consciousness. This idea could take up a full book alone, and we are not going to delve into it in great depth, but the fact remains that in everyone's consciousness, there is no room to be both grateful and negative simultaneously. I often find myself feeling grateful when I see bad in others' lives. Then it's easy to appreciate my own circumstances.

The higher level is to be grateful at all times, and it's hard. Practice being grateful. Try writing down a list of all the good things in your life, and read it a few times a day. If you can meditate for one minute on the good in your life, you can begin to protect your inner state.

Being future-focused is another strategy. When I am having difficulty with my children, I try to step back and visualize them as young adults with children of their own. In the present, they can frustrate the hell out of me, but I know their destinies will be full and great. I also am disciplined in writing down and regularly reviewing my future goals. The act of writing forces me to take ownership and solidifies the vision I have. Bear your grander intent in mind, and it will help you to remain focused.

The third strategy is to surround yourself with positive people. They will inspire you constantly—on a spiritual level, on an entrepreneurial level, and everything in between. Being with positive people is a great way to protect your confidence. Just as importantly: stay away from negative people. These people will drain you, and you will not be able to withstand the allure of the darkness. Even if they are your relatives, stay away; at Thanksgiving, sit on the opposite side of the table. If they work for you, fire them. Sometimes, these negative people come wrapped in very happy packages, so be aware. Amputation may be painful, but it is sometimes necessary.

Accentuate the Positive
Optimism is the faith that leads to achievement; nothing can be done without hope.
—Helen Keller

One technique for seeing obstacles as opportunities lies in believing in your successful future. If you are committed to staying positive and you are committed to the belief that eventually you will prevail, then success will be yours. You will be far better able to deal with the difficulties that arrive in your path. This does not, by any means, suggest that there will be an absence of obstacles. Life is hard and shit happens. You can either deal with it or quit.

Entrepreneurs choose to deal with it. Some fight their problems head-on, realizing that they must endure certain struggles to come out on the other side. Others try to simply rise above them or find a more graceful way around their obstacles. Whatever your belief, the truth remains evident: most successful people are optimistic about their own success. If you believe the economy of the world is collapsing or that our country is in a perpetual downswing, then your ability to see any obstacle as an opportunity will be greatly diminished.

The world economy is in duress. Our country is by no means perfect, but we will all struggle through this. The time to act is now. We must find the opportunities that lie hidden in the destruction. Forest fires are a catalyst for rebirth. By the same token, economic upheaval is a catalyst for change, much of which is positive.

People talk about the good old days and how things used to be better; that's the dark side tempting you. Things have never been better. Freedom of religion is pervasive in this part of the world. Infant mortality is the lowest in history. We have antibiotics to kill infections. People are living longer than they ever have. Believe in your bigger future, realize that obstacles will constantly come at you, and persevere. Deal with obstacles with a warrior's spirit, and do your best to move forward toward a great future.

TRANSFORM ADVERSITY INTO WISDOM

The ultimate measure of a man is not where he stands in moments of comfort and convenience but where he stands at times of challenge and controversy.
—Martin Luther King, Jr.

There are many obstacles that we face that we don't overcome, and ultimately, we have to pay the price for them. We can still take much away from the experience, however. We can analyze how we dealt with the problems—what worked, what didn't—and also examine the circumstances that led to the issue in the first place. This is why experienced, present, and smart people are frequently more successful than those with less experience. Instead of bouncing from one disaster to the next, successful people learn from their mistakes.

They don't repeat bad strategies, and they continue to reuse successful ones. Having the opportunity to face an obstacle is a no-lose situation if you look at it properly. You'll either kick its butt, or it'll kick yours, and you can harvest the lesson and protect yourself in the future.

When I was a much younger man, I knew a couple that lived a completely exhilarating lifestyle. They were very popular, fun to be around, and always had excitement in their lives. Eventually, I realized that there were activities going on that were not up to my moral standard. Instead of immediately distancing myself from them, though, I continued to hang out with them because it was fun; in the end, I paid a price for it. Today, I would end that relationship much faster and not put myself in that situation. That experience transformed into a learning opportunity that has benefitted me throughout the rest of my life. Bite me once, your fault. Bite me twice, my fault.

In any obstacle that you face, there exists a hidden lesson. Stay present and seek it out, and it will become your asset moving ahead on your journey. Learn from your experiences.

COMPARTMENTALIZE

One way to focus on protecting your inner state is to compartmentalize your issues. Donald Trump explained his version of this powerful technique in one of his books. Someone asked him how he could handle a nasty divorce, a major bankruptcy, and the construction of a monster casino all at the same time while still leading a happy life. Trump responded, "When I am dealing with my bankruptcy, I pull it off the shelf; and when I am done, I put it back. And in dealing with my divorce, I pull it off the shelf; when I am done, I put it back. When I am building the greatest casino of all time, I take it off the shelf; and when I am done, I put it back. I can then go out to dinner with my fantastic children and not be distracted." This technique can be learned! Use your many obligations, obstacles, and activities to help you. As you improve, you will require less time and fewer distractions to achieve this.

As you learn to compartmentalize, schedule time to focus on difficulties. Make sure there is a buffer between dealing with your dangers and focusing on your opportunities. Go to the gym. Don't walk into your house immediately after you fought with somebody—you will be a lousy father and spouse. Sit in the car, blast the radio, and clear your mind to put yourself in a better state and clear out the frustration before you walk in the house. Learning this habit is life-changing, and I wish I'd done it when I was younger.

In the Kata—the sequence of movements in Karate previously discussed in Chapter 1—one must perfect both their technique and the fluidity of their transitions. The Jumper's Success Formula comes into play here, blending greater intention, discipline, and focus to achieve those two distinct goals. As you learn to compartmentalize, try to apply a certain fluidity to your transitions. How can you go from engaging in aggressive business to walking into the house and playing with your child? Transitions, with your mind in multiple places at once, can be a dangerous period of time. Your transitions, big or small, must be tended to with focus.

✦✦✦

A great attitude does much more than turn on the lights in our worlds; it seems to magically connect us to all sorts of serendipitous opportunities that were somehow absent before the change.
—Earl Nightingale

Once again, controlling your emotional state is a key to greater life. You cannot control the world around you, but you can control how you are affected by it. Controlling this process will give you the ability to achieve so much more, and you'll be able to bring a higher level of satisfaction to your life and that of those around you. The ability to be centered will allow you to look beyond the obstacles and focus on the opportunities.

chapter 8

Build a Successful Network

Do well by doing good.
—Benjamin Franklin

I STARTED IN BUSINESS thinking that it was up to me to work hard, be smart, and accomplish a lot. I knew that I had to make money for my investors, but I really had no idea of how they fit into my intentions, nor how my friends, associates, and employees fit in. I just knew that it was up to me and about me. I realized over the course of time that my perceptions as a young entrepreneur were completely wrong. I guess I came to this realization the same way I came to the realization about love: that giving love is the best way to get it.

In the martial arts, everyone is instructed that if you want to become truly proficient, you teach others the art. True to that concept, my martial arts skills have improved significantly through teaching other people; it's forced me to create a clear vocabulary that in turn helped me understand what I was doing.

Twenty or twenty-five years ago, I had a young girl as a karate student. As her teacher, I was able to help her graduate from a white belt to a green belt. Now, she's in her forties, and she will soon receive her black belt through the coaching of a different teacher. When she sees me today, she always smiles and tells everyone, "Ben was my very first karate teacher, and I'm getting my black belt now because I loved it so much when I studied with him."

In my early business years, there were many people who helped me, and that help impacted the way I think. Some of them only helped me for their own selfish reasons, but the benefit of the help I received was no less important to me. Since then, the way I've built my business is by surrounding myself with a network of good people who are always rooting for me, always connecting me with good people, and providing guidance, support, and encouragement when I need it. I built this network by simply helping and supporting others and creating value for them both personally and professionally. Building personal and business relationships with successful, smart, or connected people is incredibly important. The good news is that it's not that hard to do it. It only takes your entire lifetime.

YOU GET WHAT YOU GIVE

Networking is simply the cultivating of mutually beneficial, give-and-take, win-win relationships. It works best, however, when emphasizing the 'give' part.
—Bob Burg

A good method for building your network is to help the people that you do business with in ways they need it. My friend Howie taught me that if you help people all the time it'll come back to you in many ways … but never in the way you expect it. Some Eastern philosophies identify this principle as karma, and it's applicable to almost every action you take. Think of the man from Chapter 5 who took the time in the middle of the night to buy gas for my wife and me. He wanted me to perform an act of kindness for someone else rather than pay him back. Karma can be applied to business as well. You get what you give, and you give what you get.

When I started in my business, I introduced my friend Jay to my cousin Phyllis. Phyllis was stuck with $500,000 worth of t-shirts and needed badly to unload them, and Jay bought them from her. I had her pay me an $8,000 commission for putting her and Jay together. I made $30,000 that year, so that was a big $8,000 for me, especially because I was just married and didn't have much money.

Today, I would never charge for helping people in businesses unrelated to mine, but I would work just as hard to put the deals together. Ultimately, helping people earns you a lot more than $8,000, and by taking money for an exchange, their emotional debt and gratitude no longer exists. When somebody pays you for a service, it's a transaction. When somebody appreciates you, a door opens up to a relationship that can be never-ending. That doesn't mean that if you don't have enough money to pay your bills, you shouldn't get paid. It only means that there is a much bigger picture than short-term profits, and it's my mission to present that picture to you. Those lessons I learned about good relationships and introductions have helped me immensely over the course of my career.

I have two warehouse projects that were my best performers before the recession hit. During the recession, they were my worst. They didn't get hit by the recession right away like my buildings with small spaces did, but by the middle of 2009, they were getting pummeled. Fortunately, I received a call from a prospective tenant for those warehouses who had heard about me from two separate sources. Those sources are people I've developed business relationships with and have helped in every way I was able to, and they were thrilled to recommend me. There is no free lunch—we make our own lunch. Go forth and make yours.

If I am not for myself, who will be for me? And if I am only for myself, what am I? And if not now, when?
—Rabbi Hillel

Every time I have a chance to separate myself from the raw commodity that I'm selling to a tenant, every time I have a chance to be measured against something beyond price per square foot, I come out ahead. Recently, a prospective tenant came to me before going to the marketplace, which meant he was interested in something more than just low rent. Ultimately, he decided to rent my property because of a personal connection. I did have to negotiate, but I was able to close the deal. That's meaningful to me. Positive emotional connections will give you a leg up every time. You must work hard to create these relationships. Sometimes your effort is for naught, but sometimes, the results of that past effort magically appear.

De-commoditizing your business is a crucial habit to develop. An emotional connection is one of the most profound ways to do this. What I mean by "de-commoditization" is simply this: if the owner of an air conditioning company wants to rent a small warehouse and he looks at three properties that are similar in appearance and location, the only difference left is the price. My job as an entrepreneur is to try and keep the decision as far away from being about the price as possible, even though my tenants will constantly try to make it so. If a tenant recommends me to their friend, or my banker recommends me to a customer, or I help a contractor with a problem and years later, he needs a space—all of these positive connections separate me from the pack and make my product more than just a commodity. The more people you can help, the luckier you will be, so be intentional about helping others.

Between 2005 and 2007, I sold four buildings. One of the tenants in those buildings, Roberto, moved into a different building that I still owned. He'd been my tenant for ten years, and when his lease expired after a decade of an honest business relationship, he chose to stay on with me. The warehouse that Roberto moved to is 36,000 square feet in total. I'd had two previous tenants, each renting 15,000 square feet, move out after a decade, and the building was struggling without tenants. Roberto rented 9,000 square feet, and it took care of almost a third of my empty space. I split the remaining space in the building into 3,000 square foot bays, and ultimately I rented them all out! That happened only because I had developed a solid business relationship with Roberto. Our relationship was not personal, but we both completely trusted each other.

And here's another strategic byproduct of this behavior: recently, out of the blue, a tenant of mine in the pharmaceutical business called me up. He is opening a new company, and because he called me first, I have a chance to rent him space. I don't know if I'm going to close the deal, but these opportunities provided to me are a sure-fire result of always trying to do the right thing. If my buildings are over-leveraged and the rents are down, I will still suffer. Recessions are still ominous and costly. Economic reality still exists; however, opportunities like renting new spaces to old tenants will help get me through the difficult times and give me a significant advantage over my competitors. Find a way to add value to your customer relationships.

You can't change the market, but you can outperform it. I am grateful for these opportunities provided by my relationships and a lifetime of good habits, honesty, and trust. Business is a two-way street—both parties need to benefit. The result is the desire for more of the same. The benefits continue into the future, and both parties' lives are greatly enhanced.

BE INVOLVED IN THE WORLD

I never wanted to go to graduate school, and my father told me I should go because of the people I would meet.

He was right. I've told my kids the same thing: to go to the best college they can go to because of the relationships they will develop with the people they'll meet in their dorm and sit next to in class. A lifetime of meeting people, developing relationships, and being involved starts right now. It only ends when you die. You network immensely in college, whether or not you know it. The guy you drink beer with today might be someone you do business with tomorrow. And, as in everything we are dealing with, if you are focused and intentional with your behavior, you'll be more successful at it. Everyone eventually meets someone that introduces them to an opportunity or to someone else who contributes to their life in some way. But we're going to do it intentionally—both in quality and quantity.

Over the last twenty years, I've been involved in many professional organizations. The Entrepreneurs' Organization (EO) is where I met young businessmen like myself. I'm a member of Vistage, where I am involved in a CEO group. I'm a member of the National Association for Industrial and Office Parks (NAIOP), where I've met hundreds of people in my market and have had many interesting educational experiences. I have hired people that I've met through NAIOP, and I've bought and sold properties as a direct result of being engaged. All of these pursuits have given me the opportunity to meet people in my local market and expand my sphere of influence. Today, I go to a ballgame or a crowded room and I always run into people I know. None of this happened by accident.

In Chapter 5, we discussed investing in charity, and I talked about the boards that I sit on and the volunteer work

I do. Keep volunteering. Keep putting yourself out there. Again, give back to the world that has given to you.

Bear in mind that the intention is not to get on the board, but to accomplish something once you get there. My friend Howie would always whisper in my ear, "What are you trying to accomplish? Are you just trying to hear yourself talk or do you have a goal in speaking?" Many people do join boards just to hear themselves talk. In my early years, I often found myself doing this. Howie showed me when to speak. He pointed out people on the board who rarely spoke, but got everything done. I learned over that fifteen-year period of being on the board that every major accomplishment gets worked out prior to the meeting, but you can only participate prior to the meeting if you have the respect and trust of the other board members. This is how politics works. There is so much for you to learn. Get involved now.

My suggestion is that you truly be engaged in the world. Be intentional, get involved, and have fun, but go in the direction of things that move you. I'm actively involved in touching a lot of lives, and through the years, it's made a lot business sense. As a result of being involved in my Jiu Jitsu school, I was introduced to four or five people that I ended up renting spaces to. When I go to the gym, I talk to the person next to me. Unsurprisingly, I meet lots of people and have fun. When I get tired of being so busy and doing all this networking, I stop and take a break. Life is a marathon, not a sprint. This is about a lifetime of behavior, not a month's worth of insanity.

The same concept applies to single people who want to meet each other and fishermen who want to find the best fishing holes in an area. These principles apply to everything in your life, and anything you do from here on out. Find ways to apply all this to your intentions. You'll get so much satisfaction from helping people—and the added benefit is that as a result of your good deeds, you get to make more money, give more charity, and get invited to even better barbecues!

FIND YOUR BALANCE

Staying home every night of the week might make you a better husband or father, but it won't make you more financially successful. Alternately, expending all of your time and energy networking with hundreds of people won't help your relationship with your family. Finding the balance between work and family is a hard conflict to reconcile. Lately, my wife and daughter have been going to mother-daughter charity events, and now they're going to chair a large event together. They've found their own activity, but it still shares common ground with mine, and they can both network and spend time together. My friend used to come home for dinner, spend some time with his children, and then go back to his office for a few hours. Everybody has to find their own way, but if you're not engaging the world, you will not avail yourself to the many opportunities that surround you. There is always a price to pay, and you have to decide if it's worth it.

Constantly be on the hunt for new relationships that open new doors. People who fish a lot have had great days on the water, but if you only go fishing twice a year, your chances for great days are minimal. The same idea can be used with people who pursue their market. You have to constantly be in an environment where you can use your expertise to help yourself or somebody else in your world. By doing this, you will find opportunities that others miss.

When my wife and I were younger and started making serious money, we started meeting people that were a lot older than us, because socially, that was natural. As we've gotten a little older, we find that we are hanging out with younger, more ambitious people. Some people are happy to enjoy their success and slow down. That takes them out of the "ambitious" category. Personally, I want to hang out with people that are ambitious and driven, like me. I find them to be much more exciting and interesting, and I get more out of those relationships. This does not negate relationships with people who were engaged and have great experience but have slowed down. Some of those people might finally have time to mentor someone now that they've retired. In order to succeed, it's important to seek out those new, fruitful relationships and get yourself exposed to the world; and it's equally important to keep in contact with people and reigniting old relationships.

BEING IN MOTION

You can have everything in life you want if you will just help enough other people get what they want.
—Zig Ziglar

We have talked a lot about the quality of your accomplishments, and about developing deep and meaningful relationships. There is also something to be said for having a significant amount of people that you are friendly with. You cannot be best friends with everyone, but if there are lots of people who you like and who like you, it makes your life better on all levels. And often, out of that pool of less deep relationships comes more meaning.

Somebody I've been on a board with is married to a woman who works for a non-profit, and their offices are moving. He called me, and I was able to introduce his wife to my partner, who is a commercial real estate broker. He found her a space and she was very happy with it. He got paid, and he was happy. I put it together, and I was happy—and now, everybody likes everybody even more. In this particular situation, more is better: more lunches, more parties, more people, more opportunities. There's more fruit in a big orchard than a small one, and we all have the power to grow our own orchard. Sometimes our competitors need to rest and miss opportunities. We won't rest as much, and we'll be there when opportunities arise—ready, primed, and able to take action because we are intentional. Be in constant motion.

One thing to add to your code of conduct: always do what you say you'll do. Follow through. If you volunteer and don't perform, you'll come across as just another schmuck, and none of this will work. A punch in karate will be powerless if it doesn't have energy behind it. Commit to things and get involved, but always follow through. Keep your promises and be a man of your word.

When you go to a football game and it's half-time, you could stay in your seat and watch the show, or you could wander around in the throng of people, looking for new friends to hang out with. Being introduced to a new friend could mean a new customer, a new mentor, or simply a new friend. You never know what you'll find, but if you look, you'll always find something. Go out and find opportunities. Don't ever stop. If you've done your preparation right, you'll be able to benefit from those opportunities. Every time you find a customer for one of your customers, every time you find someone to do business with, you are enabling your future.

One of the many results of living a life engaged is an established network of like-minded and ambitious people. After many years of pursuing this aim, I've developed something of an ecosystem where I seldom am at a loss for resources, insights, capital, endorsements, or fun.

I had a new opportunity to do some capital improvements to one of my properties at a deeply discounted rate, and for a while, I wasn't quite sure what to do. There were two basic questions I had: one based on economics and finance, and one based on the quality of the materials I wanted to buy. After half an hour of effort and phone calls to acquaintances, I had two meaningful conversations on these topics, and now I am confident on what I am going to do. Without confidence, you aren't going anywhere. My trusted network of people who have knowledge and experience allowed me to come to the conclusions I needed with ease. There are still gaps in my network, but I am always on the lookout to fill them. I do know, though, that if I need commercial financing, flooring, or air conditioning help, I can get it immediately. Meaningful and qualitative emotional support gaps are a lot harder to fill. Yet they too have to be filled. The effort you put out to accomplish this is minor in relationship to the benefits you can attain.

I have a friend, Jon, who is a new father. He was very concerned about an issue about his child. As a result of my own experience with my children, I was able to give him the confidence that everything would be okay. He found my perspective and advice to be meaningful and powerful, and he will always be appreciative of that. I was able to give him such good advice because I am fifteen years older and my kids are older, but also because I've practiced a vocabulary to communicate my experiences to an accepting ear.

In order to be able to respond to someone appropriately, you have to be able to understand their needs and communicate your thoughts in a way that moves them. Get ready to accomplish this by listening carefully—focusing—and being aware of who they are, what their path is, and what is important to them. Be in constant motion, but listen to the people around you. In this chapter, we have spoken about engaging in an active fashion and the results that follow, but I'll reiterate that listening is required to make all these connections meaningful and long-lasting. This is our only desired result. Pay attention to whom you are with when you are with someone. Listen to them and try to understand their needs. If you don't know that, you won't be able to help them in an effective way. By doing that, you will create the most important component of a powerful and long lasting network—and that is to intentionally create emotional content in these relationships.

BUILD GOOD RELATIONSHIPS WITH PROFESSIONAL RESOURCES

Building mutually beneficial relationships with the professionals and providers in your industry is crucial. In real estate, you'll have relationships with lenders, brokers and investors, heating and air conditioning companies, roofers, plumbers, electricians, painters, and lawyers. As with any other business, your relationship with your banker is critical; a good one will open you up to more financial possibilities down the road.

I bring my bank more business than most of the bank employees. They do a great job, and they deserve the added business. Recently, I brought in Mark, a guy I do business with. We'd been having lunch, and I'd asked him if he was happy with his bank. When he told me they treated him like everybody else, I seized the opportunity.

"Doesn't that suck?" I said. "I have a bank that treats you like the most successful guy in the world. Are you interested in moving your accounts?" Provided the bank can give him what he wants, he'll do it.

Bringing potential customers to my bank makes them appreciate me. If they appreciate me, they treat me better, and they help me build credibility with my customers—and they help me get the best rates that they have. They don't necessarily give me good rates because they like me—in fact, some of the senior guys might not like me at all—but because I make them money. The president of the bank and every member of the board all know that I work my butt off for this bank. I help them and talk them up to people as best

I can, and in return for my good deeds, I save money; even an extra 0.25 percent off a loan rate makes a major difference over a lifetime of borrowing.

Because I've lived by my code of conduct and paid attention to my Jumper's Success Formula, my banker wants to help me. We have a mutual admiration society that's based on helping each other whenever we can. The goal of this book is to help you do this in every aspect of your life, whether it's with your child's teacher, a nurse in the hospital, or one of your customers. If you communicate to people through your actions (rather than solely your words) that you want to help them, they will be thrilled to help you as well. How much more fun would it be living in a world where everyone around you wants to help you? Set out to do this intentionally. Work hard at it and you will surely be rewarded.

Many years ago, I bought an old flag factory with my in-laws. With 118,000 feet of empty space, the building had zero income, and the bank lent me about 60 percent of the purchase price. They made me sign personally, but I got a loan on an empty building. They would never have done that for a stranger. They only went out on a limb for me because they had confidence in me—confidence that came from years of me doing the right thing and developing the relationship. Consequently, after many years of struggling, we sold the building for a large profit, which reinforced the bank's confidence in my ability and their willingness to loan me more. As an aside, my mother-in-law made a lot of money, so she liked me better as well.

One of the goals of constantly self-improving is to make

yourself better, so that potential clients see reasons to be with you that they wouldn't otherwise see. I bring customers to the bank to open new accounts, and not only is my bank happy, but all the people I bring in are happy too. When I bring a good tenant who's been treated poorly by their bank and they get a significantly higher level of service, they are thrilled with me and I've enhanced and added value to our relationship.

Give your bank a chance to get to know you and like you; it takes time to develop a relationship. Be friends with the tellers, then meet their bosses, and get involved. With everyone you meet, you have a chance to develop a relationship. You don't have to see this as an accidental cosmic result—people will treat you the way you treat them. Acknowledge the power of karma here, and do what you can to make yours positive. We Warriors are going to intentionally make everyone we come in contact with want to become a part of our world, because we will find a way to help them or be kind to them.

You have to help people, and by helping people, you benefit yourself. A relationship you've built will one day pay off because that person will recommend you to somebody who's looking for something. You won't even know they did it, and it doesn't matter. If you live your life like everybody around you is on your team, and you love them and want to help then, then people will appreciate you and show their appreciation to you in any way they can. This is how the productive world works.

Think about the opportunity that surrounds us all if everyone we touched wanted to help us in return. It goes further, too: the people that we touch help other people, and those people come back to help us. What a nice thing. How much opportunity will come our way? It's karma and it's rational. For every action, there is an opposite and equal reaction.

Apply these concepts to your behavior and be intentional about them all. Think about how you can add value to all your business and personal relationships. By doing this, you will significantly build and enhance your network. I'm not suggesting that the only reason to be kind and loving is to get something in return, but I am suggesting that if you're intentional about being kind and loving, your returns will be exponentially greater. You will be more popular. You will be more appreciated. You will become that Warrior of Light.

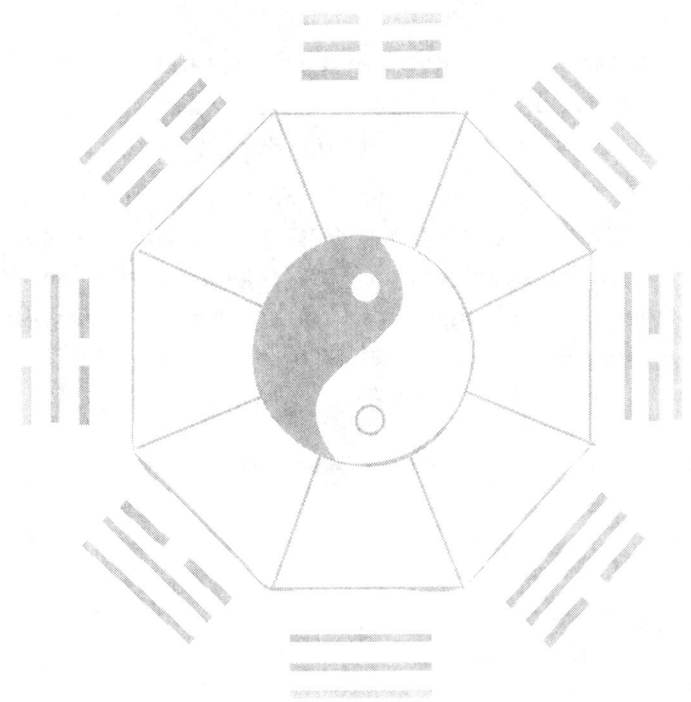

chapter 9

Being The Way:
Real Estate and Beyond

Being a warrior is not about the act of fighting. It's about being so prepared to face a challenge and believing so strongly in a cause that you are fighting for that you refuse to quit.
—Richard J. Machowicz

MY GRANDFATHER, SAM BRAUNER, came over from Europe in 1904. He was twelve years old. He got a job in the hills of Pennsylvania and eventually became a traveling salesman in a horse-drawn buggy. He met my grandmother in Pennsylvania, and when they got married, they decided to settle down and open a small store. They lived in an apartment above the store, and as their store grew, they started to fill their home with the store's inventory. My grandparents bought their store's building, expanded the store into the apartment, and moved in next door. When that apartment filled up with inventory, they expanded the store and moved again.

My grandparents always invested their money back in their business. When the Great Depression struck, money was worthless—but Sam and Sadie Brauner had goods. They had no money, but they had stockings. They had pants. They had hats. And their inventory, unlike the money in a hyper-inflated economy across the country, did not get wiped out with inflation. They continued to save by buying more inventory, real estate, and stocks.

This story passed down to me from my family was the beginning of my business philosophies. When I came into real estate, I wanted to pay down debt and own it. Over the course of the years, my philosophy on real estate has changed many times, but I've started to find my balance.

The world of real estate is my dojo; it's the only business I know. I don't know how to buy stock or companies. I'm not a doctor. I've used real estate as most of my examples for you because a primary intent of mine is to succeed—and to keep succeeding and keep improving—in the business. Understand, again, that you can apply the Jumper's Success Formula and other techniques found in this book to any area in which you wish to be successful.

As I've been striving for greatness in the world of real estate, I've received the added bonus—and accomplished another intention—of being financially successful. If you're looking for monetary success, real estate is a great option, and it's one that you can include along with your other goals. You could make money buying and selling shoes, and use that profit to invest in real estate. You could be an orthopedic surgeon, or a periodontist like my brother David, and make a lot of money both being a doctor and investing in real estate.

It took years to get to where I am today, and I've certainly made mistakes. Real estate can be a world of risk sometimes—you have absolutely no control over what the economy is going to do while you're playing in it. Now, in 2013, I think it's a good day to buy real estate. But 2005-2007 were probably some of the worst years to do so.

In 2007, I sold a few properties, because some buyers offered me more money than my buildings were worth. In hindsight, I should probably have sold everything in 2007, because the recession hit, and by 2009, my properties were worth half of what they were worth in 2007.

I used the money from those sales to start a lending business. I targeted customers with bad credit, and I loaned them money on real estate. I thought I was a genius because if all had gone according to plan, I would have made 12 percent on my money. Ultimately, though, most of those people never paid me back, and I had to foreclose on some properties that were worth pennies on the dollar. I lost millions.

I got my butt kicked, I got brutalized, and I got hurt badly. I thought I was so smart at the time that I was doing loans on properties that I hadn't even looked at. I did loans on properties in Las Vegas and Arizona and northern Florida—places I had no experience in. My reasoning was simple: there was a building boom, and every piece of ground was worth a fortune. But as soon as that home building craze stopped, those properties dropped 80 percent in value, and there I was, having spent twenty years making money and two years giving it all away.

I did not lose money on properties I owned where I knew what I was doing. I was conservative in my core business, so that when I did make all of those mistakes, I had something great to fall back on. Even with that safety net, though, I crashed as hard as the market had; I no longer felt successful in the world that I'd previously been so competent at managing. I hadn't reached my goal. I'd failed.

In hindsight, I'm grateful for those hard times. It was one of many experiences that taught me valuable lessons so that I could get to where I am now. I made many mistakes because I got haughty. I became over-confident. Eventually, I came to the realization that I didn't like feeling like a failure, and when my wife called me a pussy, I'd had enough. I went to work every day, and I focused on saving my life. I renewed my focus on being a champion. In 1991, when I first started from scratch in real estate, I focused on being great and successful and getting deals done. I had my sword and my shield in my hand, and I was charging forward. In 2009, I lost my mojo, and I was simply scared. I had to focus on doing the right thing.

So I did it. I lowered people's rents to keep my tenants on when their leases ended. I struggled to cut expenses. I did whatever I could do to make it work. I was uncomfortable and unhappy, and it took a lot of focus and commitment to not allow my insecurities to conquer me during that time. Slowly but surely, I got out of it. I fought with everything I had. I started to think about being intentional again, and the world opened up for me.

◆◆◆

Sometimes you have to play a long time to be able to play like yourself.
—Miles Davis

It took years of both experience and mistakes to get to where I am today. As you're playing in your dojo, you learn how to craft a philosophy and a method of focusing. Your philosophies and intentions will change over time, and they should—remember, the only certainty in life besides death is change. You'll get older, your experiences will grow, your health will shift, the economy will have its ups and downs. But you always need to have intention and direction along The Way.

There are no specific answers for anything. But if you're always focused on studying the market and disciplined about improving yourself and intent on doing the right thing, you're close; if you're taking people out to dinner and developing relationships and networking and volunteering—all these guidelines I've given you will ultimately lead you to being capable of getting a good deal and getting it done. Being a lifetime learner will get you there, so will being focused in your commitment to meeting people, to knowing what's going on in your field, to being honest, to being self-aware. All of these things will get you there.

◆◆◆

Today, I go to work excited. I'm growing again. I have phenomenal employees that I trust. I'm working on five or six deals, and I have no idea which one I'll get, but I'm doing it! My reputation is helping me relate to people, my banks like me, and I'm having fun. The fun is the best part about business for me, and interestingly, it's not about the money so much as that struggle, that reaching for my goals with passion and intention. If you can focus on doing something that you love and are passionate about, life can be fantastic. And when you go home to the family that loves you, that wonder and passion spills over to your love for them. They react positively, and then all of a sudden you're having a great time at home! The joy, the passion, the wonder, the positivity—all of it spills over into the next area of your life, and the next.

I know this feeling of euphoria won't last forever. There will be frustrating times and difficult challenges. I'm human, and I screw up. Everyone does. My wife calls me her knight in dented, rusty armor, because I'm out there trying to fight the good fight, but I sure as hell am not smooth or clean all the time. Failure is an expected part of life. I know, though, that every time I apply this stuff that works, my perspective changes. It gets better and better. *And if I could just manifest this feeling all the time in every single aspect of my life, everything would be greater.*

If.

If

If you can keep your head when all about you
Are losing theirs and blaming it on you,
If you can trust yourself when all men doubt you,
But make allowance for their doubting too;
If you can wait and not be tired by waiting,
Or being lied about, don't deal in lies,
Or being hated don't give way to hating,
And yet don't look too good, nor talk too wise:

If you can dream—and not make dreams your master;
If you can think—and not make thoughts your aim,
If you can meet with Triumph and Disaster
And treat those two impostors just the same;
If you can bear to hear the truth you've spoken
Twisted by knaves to make a trap for fools,
Or watch the things you gave your life to, broken,
And stoop and build 'em up with worn-out tools:

If you can make one heap of all your winnings
And risk it on one turn of pitch-and-toss,
And lose, and start again at your beginnings
And never breathe a word about your loss;
If you can force your heart and nerve and sinew
To serve your turn long after they are gone,
And so hold on when there is nothing in you
Except the Will which says to them: "Hold on!"

If you can talk with crowds and keep your virtue,
Or walk with Kings—nor lose the common touch,
If neither foes nor loving friends can hurt you,
If all men count with you, but none too much;
If you can fill the unforgiving minute
With sixty seconds' worth of distance run,
Yours is the Earth and everything that's in it,
And—which is more—you'll be a Man, my son!
　　　　—Rudyard Kipling

A big thank you to Jon LoDuca.
He is a good friend and has wonderful entrepreneurial insight.
His ability to create rational thought from chaos
helped to guide me throughout the writing of this book.

Thank you, Jon.

CPSIA information can be obtained
at www.ICGtesting.com
Printed in the USA
FFOW03n1937220817
39144FF